WebRTC

APIs and RTCWEB Protocols of the
HTML5 Real-Time Web

WebRTC

APIs and RTCWEB Protocols of the
HTML5 Real-Time Web

Alan B. Johnston

Daniel C. Burnett

First Edition
September 2012

C:

Digital Codex LLC

∅∅∅∅

ISBN-13:978-0985978808
ISBN-10: 0985978805

DEDICATION

For Aidan & Nora, and Craig & Fiona

TABLE OF CONTENTS

LIST OF FIGURES AND TABLES

ACKNOWLEDGMENTS

We would like to thank our technical reviewers Alex Agranovsky, Carol Davids, David Kemp, Henry Sinnreich, Harvey Waxman, and Dan York. We would also like to thank Marina Burnett and Chris Comfort for their proofreading and comments. We would also like to thank our families for their encouragement and support.

And finally, we would like to acknowledge our colleagues in W3C and the IETF who are working incredibly hard at creating the WebRTC standards.

PREFACE

The Internet and the World Wide Web have changed our world. When the history of this period is written, much will be said about the impact of these technologies on life in the late 20th and early 21st centuries. The web has changed the way we receive information, interact with others, work, and play. Now, the web is about to dramatically change the way we communicate using voice and video. This book gives an up-to-the-minute snapshot of the standards and industry effort known as WebRTC, which is short for Web Real-Time Communications. This technology, along with other advances in HTML5 browsers, has the potential to revolutionize the way we all communicate, in both personal and business spheres.

The authors have been involved in the Internet Communications industry for many years, and have seen the advances and impact of the Internet on voice and video communications. We have worked on signaling protocols such as Session Initiation Protocol (SIP), Session Description Protocol (SDP), and security protocols such as ZRTP for voice and video communication systems that will form the basis of what will inevitably replace the telephone system (called the Public Switched Telephone Network or PSTN). These Internet Communications technologies have brought an amazing wave of disruption, but we believe WebRTC has the potential to create even greater disruption.

This book provides information for web developers and telephony developers who want to catch this new wave while it is still building. The standards and protocols needed for WebRTC are still being developed and invented. Browsers are starting to support WebRTC functionality, little by little. However, the authors have seen the need for a book to explain this still-developing technology. This book will explain the technical goals, architectures, protocols, and Application Programming Interfaces (APIs) of WebRTC. In a publishing experiment, we plan to produce frequent editions of this book, perhaps as often as three per year, and focus on digital delivery and on-demand publishing to keep costs down and for maximum hyper linking usefulness. For information on the latest edition and for a list of updates and changes, visit http://webrtcbook.com.

This book begins with an introduction to WebRTC and discusses what is new about it. The unique aspects of WebRTC peer-to-peer media flows are explored, and Network Address Translation (NAT) traversal explained. We then discuss the working documents and finalized documents that together comprise the WebRTC standards-in-progress in both the World Wide Web Consortium (W3C) and the Internet Engineering Task Force (IETF). Each chapter ends with a references section, listing the various standards documents. References of the form [RFC...] are IETF Request For Comments documents. References of the form [draft-...] are IETF Internet-Drafts, working documents, whose content may have been updated or changed since the publication of this book. The hyperlinks provided will, in most cases, retrieve the most recent version of the document. References to W3C drafts include a link to the latest public working draft, and also a link to the latest editor's draft. For those of you unfamiliar with the standardization processes of W3C and the IETF, we have provided a reference in Appendices A and B. Finally, we discuss the current state of deployment in popular browsers.

If you are a web developer, welcome to the world of Internet Communications! Your users will greatly enjoy the ability to interact with each other using your application's real-time voice and video capabilities. To understand our descriptions of APIs, you will need a working knowledge of HTML and JavaScript, and some experience in web applications. See Appendix D for some useful references for this.

If you are a VoIP or telephony developer, welcome to the web world! Your users will enjoy the capabilities of high quality audio and video communication, and rich, web-powered user interfaces. To understand our descriptions of the on-the-wire protocols for transporting voice, video, and data, you will need a basic understanding of the Internet. Knowledge of another Internet Communication signaling protocol such as SIP or Jingle is also useful. See Appendix D for some additional useful reference reading.

In many ways, WebRTC is a merging of worlds between the web and telephony. To help bridge the gap between the web and telephony world, we have also included a Glossary in Appendix C to briefly explain some common terms and concepts from each world.

The authors look forward to participating in the next wave of disruption and innovation that WebRTC will likely unleash.

We would love to hear from you and interact with you on Twitter (@alanbjohnston and @danielcburnett) or on Google+ (alanbjohnston@gmail.com and danielcburnett@gmail.com).

1 INTRODUCTION TO WEB REAL-TIME COMMUNICATIONS

Web Real-Time Communications (RTC), or WebRTC, adds new functionality to the web browser. For the first time, browsers will interact directly with other browsers, resulting in a number of architectures including a triangle and trapezoid model. The media capabilities of WebRTC are state-of-the-art, with many new features. The underlying standards of WebRTC are being developed by the World Wide Web Consortium (W3C) and the Internet Engineering Task Force (IETF).

1.1 WebRTC Introduction

WebRTC is an industry and standards effort to put real-time communications capabilities into all browsers and make these capabilities accessible to web developers via standard [HTML5] tags and JavaScript APIs (Application Programming Interfaces). For example, consider functionality similar to that offered by Skype™ [SKYPE] but without having to install any software or plug-ins. For a website or web application to work regardless of which browser is used, standards are required. Also, standards are required so that browsers can communicate with non-browsers, including enterprise and service provider telephony and communications equipment.

1.1.1 The Web Browsing Model

The basic model of web applications is shown in Figure 1.1. Transport of information between the browser and the web server is provided by the Hyper-Text Transport Protocol, HTTP (Section 5.2.1), which runs over Transmission Control Protocol, TCP (Section 5.2.8), or in some new

1

implementations, over the WebSocket protocol (see Section 5.2.12). The content or application is carried in Hyper-Text Markup Language, HTML, which typically includes JavaScript and Cascading Style Sheets [CSS]. In the simple case, the browser sends an HTTP request to the web server for content, and the web server sends a response containing the document or image or other information requested. In the more complex case, the server sends JavaScript which runs on the browser, interacting with the browser through APIs and with the user through clicks and selects. The browser exchanges information with the server through an open HTTP or WebSockets channel.

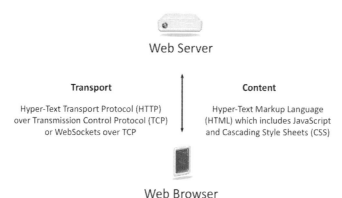

Web Server

Transport		Content
Hyper-Text Transport Protocol (HTTP) over Transmission Control Protocol (TCP) or WebSockets over TCP		Hyper-Text Markup Language (HTML) which includes JavaScript and Cascading Style Sheets (CSS)

Web Browser

Figure 1.1 Web Browser Model

In figures in this book, we will show an arrow between the web browser and the web server to indicate the web session between them. Since WebRTC can utilize any web transport, the details of this connection, and whether it is HTTP or WebSockets is not discussed.

1.1.2 The Real-Time Communication Function in the Browser

Figure 1.2 shows the browser model and the role of the real-time communication function. The lighter block called "Browser RTC Function" is the focus of this book. The unique nature and requirements of real-time communications means that adding and standardizing this block is non-trivial. The RTC function interacts with the web application using standard APIs. It communicates with the Operating System using the browser. A new aspect of WebRTC is the interaction that occurs browser-to-browser, known as a "Peer Connection", where the RTC Function in one browser communicates using on-the-wire standard protocols (not HTTP) with the RTC Function in another browser or Voice over IP (VoIP) or video application. While web traffic uses TCP for transport, the on-the-wire protocol between browsers can use other transport protocols such as

User Datagram Protocol, UDP.

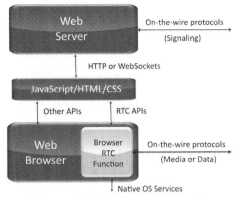

Figure 1.2 The Browser Model

1.1.3 Elements of a WebRTC System

Figure 1.3 shows a typical set of elements in a WebRTC system. This includes web servers, browsers running various operating systems on various devices including desktop PCs, tablets, and mobile phones, and other servers. Additional elements include gateways to the Public Switched Telephone Network (PSTN) and other Internet communication endpoints such as Session Initiation Protocol (SIP) phones and clients or Jingle clients. WebRTC enables communication among all these devices. The figures in this book will use these icons and elements as examples.

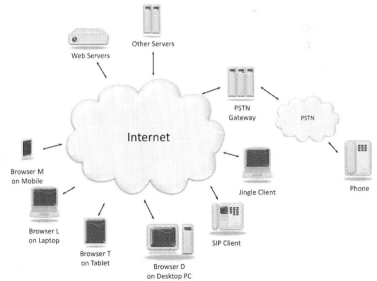

Figure 1.3 Elements in a WebRTC Environment

1.1.4 The WebRTC Triangle

Initially, the most common scenario is likely to be where both browsers are running the same WebRTC web application, downloaded from the same webpage. This produces the WebRTC "Triangle" shown in Figure 1.4. This arrangement is called a triangle due to the shape of the signaling (sides of triangle) and media or data flows (base of triangle) between the three elements. A Peer Connection establishes the transport for voice and video media and data channel flows directly between the browsers.

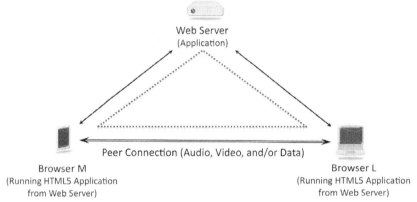

Web Server
(Application)

Peer Connection (Audio, Video, and/or Data)

Browser M
(Running HTML5 Application
from Web Server)

Browser L
(Running HTML5 Application
from Web Server)

Figure 1.4 The WebRTC "Triangle"

Note that while we sometimes refer to the connection between the browser and server as signaling, it is not really signaling as used in telephony systems. Signaling is not standardized in WebRTC as it is just considered part of the application. This signaling may run over HTTP or WebSockets to the same web server that serves HTML pages to the browser, or to a completely different web server that just handles the signaling.

1.1.5 The WebRTC Trapezoid

Figure 1.5 shows the WebRTC Trapezoid [draft-ietf-rtcweb-overview], based on the SIP Trapezoid [RFC 3261]. The two web servers are shown communicating using a standard signaling protocol such as Session Initiation Protocol (SIP), used by many VoIP and video conferencing systems, or Jingle [XEP-0166], used to add voice and video capability to Jabber [RFC 6120] instant messaging and presence systems. Alternatively, a proprietary signaling protocol could be used. Note that in these more complicated cases, the media may not flow directly between the two browsers, but may go through media relays and other elements, as discussed in Chapter 3.

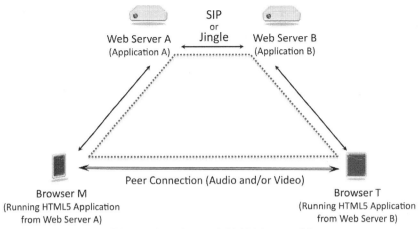

Figure 1.5 The WebRTC Trapezoid

1.1.6 WebRTC and the Session Initiation Protocol (SIP)

Figure 1.6 shows WebRTC interoperating with SIP. The Web Server has a built-in SIP signaling gateway to allow the call setup information to be exchanged between the browser and the SIP client. The resulting media flow is directly between the browser and the SIP client, as the Peer Connection establishes a standard Real-time Transport Protocol (RTP) media session (Section 5.2.2) with the SIP User Agent. Other ways of interoperating with SIP are covered in Section 2.2.6.

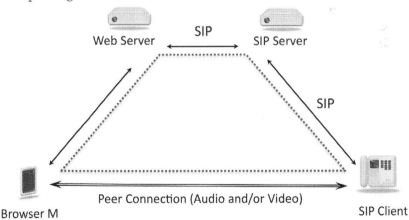

Figure 1.6 WebRTC Interoperating with SIP

1.1.7 WebRTC and Jingle

Figure 1.7 shows how WebRTC can interoperate with Jingle. The Web Server has a built-in Extensible Messaging and Presence Protocol, XMPP [RFC 6120], also known as Jabber, server which talks through another XMPP server to a Jingle client.

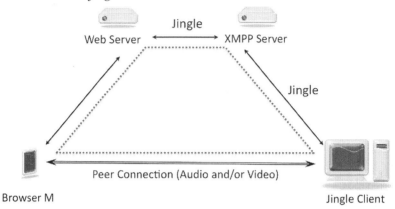

Figure 1.7 WebRTC Interoperating with Jingle

1.1.8 WebRTC and the Public Switched Telephone Network (PSTN)

Figure 1.8 shows how WebRTC can interoperate with the Public Switched Telephone Network (PSTN). The PSTN Gateway terminates the audio-only media stream and connects the PSTN telephone call with the media. Some sort of signaling is needed between the Web Server and the PSTN Gateway. It could be SIP, or a master/slave control protocol.

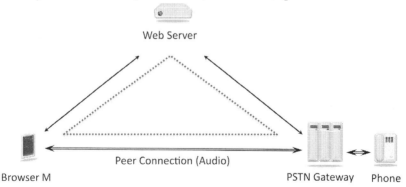

Figure 1.8 WebRTC Interoperating with the PSTN

It is not expected that browsers will be assigned telephone numbers or be part of the PSTN. Instead, an Internet Communication service could assign a telephone number to a user, and that user could use WebRTC to access the service. As a result, a telephone call to that PSTN number wo "ring" the browser and an answered call would result in an audio session across the Internet connected to the PSTN caller. Other services could include the ability to "dial" a telephone number in a WebRTC application which would result in the audio path across the Internet to the PSTN.

Note that the phone in Figure 1.8 could be a normal PSTN phone ("landline" or "black phone") or a mobile phone. The fact that it might be running VoLTE (Voice over Long Term Evolution) or other VoIP (Voice over Internet Protocol) protocol doesn't change this picture, as the Peer Connection will terminate with a VoIP gateway.

Another interesting area is the role of WebRTC in providing emergency services. While a WebRTC service could support emergency calling in the same way as VoIP Internet Communication services, there is the potential that the Public Service Answering Point (PSAP) could become a WebRTC application, and answer emergency "calls" directly from other browsers, completely bypassing the PSTN. Of course, this raises all kinds of interesting security, privacy, and jurisdiction issues.

1.2 Multiple Media Streams in WebRTC

Devices today can generate and consume multiple media types and multiple streams of each type. Even in the simple point-to-point example shown in Figure 1.9, a mobile phone and a desktop PC could generate a total of six media streams. For multiparty sessions, this number will be much higher. As a result, WebRTC has built-in capabilities for dealing with multiple media streams and sources.

Figure 1.9 Multiple Media Streams in a Point-to-Point WebRTC Session

1.3 Multi-Party Sessions in WebRTC

The preceding examples have been point-to-point sessions between two browsers, or between a browser and another endpoint. WebRTC also supports multi-party or conferencing sessions involving multiple browsers.

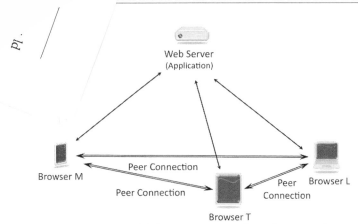

Figure 1.10 Multiple Peer Connections Between Browsers

One way to do this is to have each browser establish a Peer Connection with the other browsers in the session. This is shown in Figure 1.10. This is sometimes referred to as a "full mesh" or "fully distributed" conferencing architecture. Each browser establishes a full mesh of Peer Connections with the other browsers. For audio media, this might mean mixing the media received from each browser. For video, this might mean rendering the video streams from other browsers to different windows with appropriate labeling. As new browsers join the session, new Peer Connections are established to send and receive the new media streams.

An alternative architecture to the full-mesh model of Figure 1.10 is also possible with WebRTC. For a multiple browser conference, a centralized media server/mixer/selector can be used; this requires only a single Peer Connection to be established between each browser and the media server. This is shown in Figure 1.11. This is sometimes referred to as a "centrally mixed" conferencing architecture. Each browser sends media to the server, which distributes it to the other browsers, with or without mixing. From the perspective of browser M, media streams from browser L and T are received over a single Peer Connection from the server. As new browsers join the session, no new Peer Connections involving browser M need to be established. Instead, new media streams are received over the existing Peer Connection between browser M and the media server.

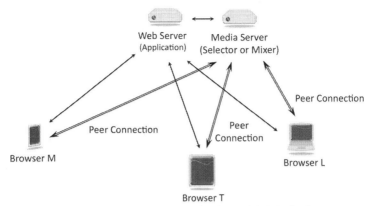

Figure 1.11 Single Peer Connection with Media Server

The full-mesh architecture of Figure 1.10 has the advantages of no media server infrastructure, and lowest media latency and highest quality. However, this architecture may not be suitable for a large multi-party conference because the bandwidth required at each browser grows with each new participant. The centralized architecture of Figure 1.11 has the advantage of being able to scale to very large sessions while also minimizing the amount of processing needed by each browser when a new participant joins the session, although it is perhaps inefficient when only one or a small number of browsers are involved, such as in peer-to-peer gaming.

1.4 WebRTC Standards

The WebRTC standards are currently under joint development by the World Wide Web Consortium (W3C) [W3C] and the Internet Engineering Task Force (IETF) [IETF]. W3C is working on defining the APIs needed for JavaScript web applications to interact with the browser RTC function. These APIs, such as the Peer Connection API, are described in Chapter 4. The IETF is developing the protocols used by the browser RTC function to talk to another browser or Internet Communications endpoint. These protocols, for example, extensions to the Real-time Transport Protocol, are described in Chapter 5.

There are pre-standard implementations of many of the components of WebRTC in some browsers today. See Chapter 8 for details.

Note that there is an important distinction between 'pre-standard' and 'proprietary' implementations. Pre-standard implementations emerge during the development stage of standards, and are critical to gain experience and information before standards are finalized and locked down. Pre-standard implementations often follow an early or draft version of the standards, or partially implement standards as a 'proof of concept'. Once the standard has been finalized, these pre-standard implementations must move towards the standards, or else they risk becoming a proprietary implementation. Proprietary implementations fragment the user and development base, which in an area such as communications can greatly reduce the value of the services.

The W3C work is centered around the WEBRTC Working Group and the IETF work is centered around the RTCWEB (Real-Time Communications Web) Working Group. The two groups are independent, but closely coordinate together and have many common participants, including the authors.

The projected time frame for publication of the first version of standards in the IETF is the second half of 2012 and for W3C in early 2013. However, these dates are most likely overly optimistic. (When do engineers ever realistically estimate level of effort?) Standards-compliant WebRTC browsers are expected to be generally available sometime in 2013.

1.5 What is New in WebRTC

There are many new and exciting capabilities in WebRTC that are not available even in today's VoIP and video conferencing systems. Some of these features are listed in Table 1.1. The rest of this book will explain how these are achieved using the WebRTC APIs and protocols.

1.6 Important Terminology Notes

In this book, when we refer to the entire effort to add standardized communication capabilities into browsers, we shall use WebRTC. When we are referring to the W3C Working Group, we will use WEBRTC. When we are referring to the IETF Working Group, we will use RTCWEB. Note that WebRTC is also used to describe the Google/Mozilla open source media engine [WEBRTC.ORG], which is an implementation of WebRTC.

In addition, because the main W3C specification is titled "The WebRTC Specification" [WEBRTC 1.0], we use its full title to reference this particular W3C document, which is a key part of WebRTC, but by no means the entire specification.

Also note that the World Wide Consortium refers to itself as "W3C" and not "the W3C". We have adopted this convention throughout this book.

Feature	Provided Using	Why Important
Platform and device independence	Standard APIs from W3C, standard protocols from IETF	Developers can write WebRTC HTML5 code that will run across different OS, browsers, and devices, desktop and mobile.
Secure voice and video	Secure RTP Protocol (SRTP) encryption and authentication	Browsers are used in different environments and over unsecured WiFi networks. Encryption means that others can't listen in or record voice or video.
Advanced voice and video quality	Opus audio codec, VP8 video codec, and others	Having built-in standard codecs ensures interoperability and avoids codec downloads, a way malicious sites install spyware and viruses. New codecs can adapt when congestion is detected.
Reliable session establishment	Hole punching through Network Address Translation (NAT)	Direct media between browsers is noticeably more reliable and better quality than server-relayed media. Also, the load on servers is reduced.
Multiple media streams and media types sent over a single transport	Real-time Transport Protocol (RTP) and Session Description Protocol (SDP) extensions	Establishing direct media using hole punching can take time. Sending all media over a single session is also more efficient and reliable.
Adaptive to network conditions	Multiplexed RTP Control Protocol (RTCP), Secure Audio Video Profile with Feedback (SAVPF)	Feedback on network conditions is essential for video, and will be especially important for the high definition, high bandwidth sessions in WebRTC.
Support for multiple media types and multiple sources of media	APIs and signaling to negotiate size/format of each source individually	The ability to negotiate each individually results in most efficient use of bandwidth and other resources.
Interoperability with VoIP and video communication systems using SIP, Jingle, and PSTN	Standard Secure RTP (SRTP) media, Standard SDP and extensions	Existing VoIP and video systems can work with new WebRTC systems using standard protocols.

Table 1.1 New Features of WebRTC

1.7 References

[HTML5]   http://www.w3.org/TR/html5

[SKYPE]   http://www.skype.com

[CSS]   http://www.w3.org/Style/CSS

[draft-ietf-rtcweb-overview]   http://tools.ietf.org/html/draft-ietf-rtcweb-overview

[RFC 3261]   http://tools.ietf.org/html/rfc3261

[XEP-0166]   http://xmpp.org/extensions/xep-0166.html

[RFC 6120]   http://tools.ietf.org/html/rfc6120

[W3C]   http://www.w3c.org

[IETF]   http://www.ietf.org

[WEBRTC.ORG]   http://www.webrtc.org

[WEBRTC 1.0]   http://www.w3.org/TR/webrtc

2 HOW TO USE WEBRTC

WebRTC is easy to use, with just a few steps necessary to establish media sessions. A number of messages flow between the browser and the server, while others flow directly between the two browsers, known as peers. WebRTC can even establish sessions with SIP, Jingle, and PSTN endpoints. There are many standards involved in the WebRTC effort - so many that it can be difficult to know where to start when learning about it. Since many readers of this text will likely be developers of WebRTC applications, the following sections give an overview of how to set up a WebRTC session, what can be done while the session is running, and how to close down the session. WebRTC can be used in a number of different architectures. Example pseudo code illustrates the operation of the WebRTC APIs.

2.1 Setting Up a WebRTC Session

As an application developer, the three main actions to take when setting up a WebRTC session are:

1) Obtain local media,
2) Set up a connection between the browser and the peer (other browser or endpoint), and
3) Attach media and data channels to the connection.

The details of how to do these three steps in WebRTC are shown in Figure 2.1. Note that this figure corresponds with Figure 1.4.

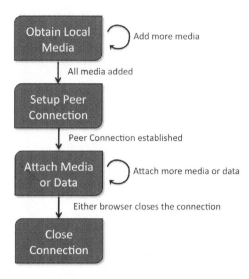

Figure 2.1 WebRTC Session Establishment, API View

The following subsections briefly describe each of these steps, as well as the process for closing down a session when complete.

2.1.1 Obtaining Local Media

There are a variety of ways to obtain media, the complete list of which is out of scope for this book. However, one of the most common ways is defined by the WebRTC effort: `getUserMedia()` (Section 4.3.2). This method can be used to obtain a single `LocalMediaStream`. Once you have one or more media streams, you can piece them together into the streams you want using the `MediaStream` API (Application Programming Interface). For privacy reasons, a web application's request for access to a user's microphone or camera will only be granted after the browser has obtained permission from the user.

2.1.2 Setting up the Peer Connection

Another important step is to set up the Peer Connection using the API by the same name. The core of WebRTC is the `RTCPeerConnection` API, which, as its name suggests, sets up a connection between two Peers. In this context, "peers" means two communication endpoints on the World Wide Web, as in the phrase "peer-to-peer file sharing". Instead of requiring communication through a server, the communication is direct between the two entities. In the specific case of WebRTC, a Peer Connection is a direct media connection between two web browsers. This is particularly relevant when a multi-way communication such as a conference call is set up among three or more browsers. Each pair of browsers will require a single Peer Connection to join them, allowing for audio and video media to flow directly between the two, as shown in Figure 1.10. Thus, three browsers communicating would need a total of three connections among them. An application developer will need to set up one Peer Connection per pair of browsers (or a browser and another endpoint such as an existing communications network) being connected. The alternative architecture of Figure 1.11 is also possible.

To establish this connection requires a new `RTCPeerConnection` object. The only input to the `RTCPeerConnection` constructor method is a configuration object containing the information that ICE, Interactive Connectivity Establishment (Section 5.2.4), will use to "punch holes" through intervening Network Address Translation (NAT) devices and firewalls.

2.1.3 Exchanging Media or Data

Once the connection is set up, any number of local media streams may be attached to the Peer Connection for sending across the connection to the remote browser. Similarly, any number of remote media streams may also be sent to the local end of the connection, resulting in new media streams at the local end that may be manipulated just like any other local media stream.

It is important to note that every change in media requires a negotiation (or renegotiation) between browsers of how media will be represented on the channel. When a request is made, locally or remotely, to add or remove media, the browser can be asked to generate an appropriate `SessionDescription` object (a container for a session description – information about how to establish the media session) to represent the complete set of media flowing over the Peer Connection. The `RTCPeerConnection` API provides a means by which the application author can view and edit (if desired) the session description before it is sent to the remote side. This design allows the browser to handle the "heavy lifting" of proposing codecs and writing Session Description Protocol (SDP), Section 5.2.3, used to represent the session description, while still allowing for minor adjustments by the application as needed. However, it is expected that in the majority of cases, the web developer will not need to modify or inspect `SessionDescription` objects.

Once the browsers have exchanged `SessionDescription` objects, the media or data session can be established. Both browsers begin hole punching. Once hole punching completes, key negotiation for the secure media session can begin. Finally, the media or data session can begin. Note that all of this activity, everything after the `SessionDescription` objects

15

have been exchanged, is done by the browser on behalf of the JavaScript code. The application JavaScript code may add or remove STUN and TURN servers, Sections 5.2.5 and 5.2.6, used for NAT traversal and monitor the process, but the work is done by the browser.

2.1.4 Closing the Connection

Either browser can close the connection. The application calls `close()` on the `RTCPeerConnection` object to indicate that it is finished using the connection, perhaps in response to a user clicking a button or closing a tab. This causes ICE processing and media streaming to stop. Similarly, should one browser lose Internet connectivity, or crash, the keep-alives sent in the media or data channel will fail, and the other browser will attempt to restart hole punching, and when that fails close the session. Once the session is over, the browser removes any session-granted permissions to access the microphone and camera of the device, so a new session will require new permission(s) from the user.

2.2 WebRTC Example Implementations

The following sections will show some examples of WebRTC implementations. Figure 2.2 shows a protocol view of WebRTC Session Establishment.

The following figures provide more details of the protocol exchanges, using "ladder diagrams", sometimes called call flows.

Protocols such as SRTP, SDP, and ICE are introduced in Chapter 5.

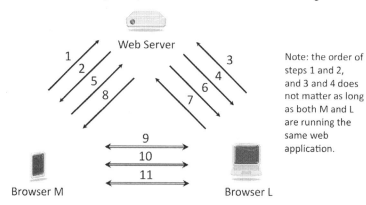

1) Browser M requests web page from web server
2) Web sever provides web pages to M with WebRTC JavaScript
3) Browser L requests web page from web server
4) Web sever provides web pages to L with WebRTC JavaScript
5) M decides to communicate with L, JavaScript on M causes M's session description object (offer) to be sent to the web server

16

6) Web server sends M's session description object to the JavaScript on L
7) JavaScript on L causes L's session description object (answer) to be sent to web server
8) Web server sends L's session description object to the JavaScript on M
9) M and L begin hole punching to determine the best way to reach the other browser
10) After hole punching completes, M and L begin key negotiation for secure media
11) M and L begin exchanging voice, video, or data

Figure 2.2 WebRTC Session Establishment, Protocol View

2.2.1 Session Establishment in WebRTC Triangle

Basic session establishment with WebRTC is shown in Figure 2.3. Note that this figure corresponds with Figure 2.2.

Browsers M and L are running the same WebRTC enabled JavaScript downloaded from the web server. When one user wishes to communicate with another user, this begins the media negotiation between the browsers, referred to as an offer/answer exchange.

Media negotiation is the way in which two parties in a communication session, such as two browsers, communicate and come to agreement on an acceptable media session. Offer/answer is an approach to media negotiation in which one party first sends to the other party what media types and capabilities it supports and would like to establish – this is known as the "offer". The other party then responds indicating which of the offered media types and capabilities are supported and acceptable for this session – this is known as the "answer". This process can be repeated a number of times to setup and modify a session, for example to add new media streams or to change which streams are to be sent. A common question is why this back-and-forth process is needed, rather than, for example, each side merely stating what it intends to do. The primary reason is to ensure that both sides have agreement before media begins flowing. This is crucial for the lower layers in the browser that may not be able to handle media that comes in before the browser is ready for it.

In addition to offers and answers, there is also a "provisional answer" (pranswer). A provisional answer is an answer to an offer, but it is provisional or tentative. It may not be the final answer given in the actual answer, which comes later in the offer/answer exchange. Provisional answers are optional, and in general will only occur when interoperating with the PSTN or some VoIP systems that emulate the "early media" characteristics of the telephone network.

When the user on browser M decides to communicate with the user on browser L, the JavaScript on browser M provides a constraint-based description of the media it wants, requests the media, and gets user permission. It is important that the permission grant is tied to the domain of the web page, and that this permission does not extend to pop-ups and other frames on the web page. The desired media session information is captured in a session description object. This is the offer, which is sent to browser L through the web server. It is important to note that WebRTC does not standardize how browser M sends this offer to browser L. There are a number of ways in which this could be accomplished, such as XML HTTP Request [XHR]. Browser L receives the session description object offer and generates a session description object answer, which is sent back to browser M using the same method. Once the offer/answer exchange is complete, hole punching (and key negotiation) can begin, and eventually the exchange of media packets.

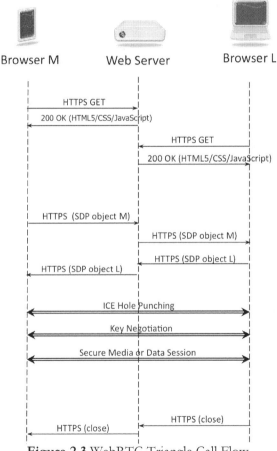

Figure 2.3 WebRTC Triangle Call Flow

18

Browser L closes the connection, which causes the Peer Connection to be closed and all permissions for microphone and cameras.

2.2.2 Session Establishment in WebRTC Trapezoid

The call flow for the WebRTC Trapezoid of Figure 1.5 is shown in Figure 2.4 below.

In this scenario, browsers M and L exchange media directly, despite running web applications from different web servers. The session description objects from each browser are mapped to a Jingle [XEP-0166] session-initiate message and session-accept method. Currently, the defined mapping of Jingle to and from Session Description Protocol [XEP-0167] does not include the WebRTC extensions and attributes of SDP, but it could be extended to do so.

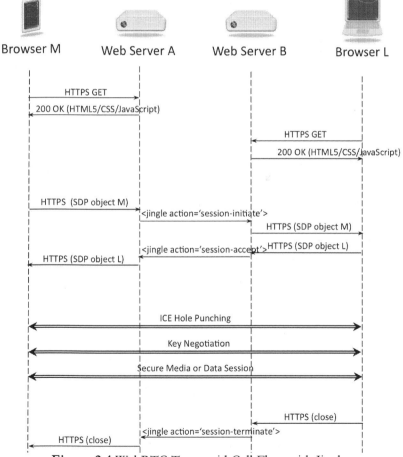

Figure 2.4 WebRTC Trapezoid Call Flow with Jingle

Note that this scenario could alternatively have mapped the session description objects to SDP and used SIP signaling between the browsers. No changes to the SIP protocol are needed to do this.

2.2.3 WebRTC Session Establishment with SIP Endpoint

WebRTC interworking with SIP [RFC 3261] is shown in detail in Figure 2.5 below. This corresponds with Figure 1.4. WebRTC defines the mapping of the session description object offers and answers to SIP, which can be carried without modification or extension in normal SIP INVITE and 200 OK messages.

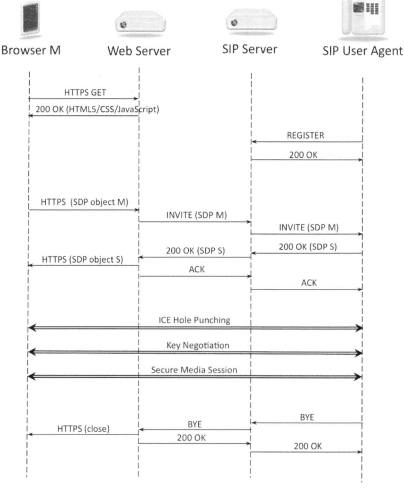

Figure 2.5 WebRTC Interoperating with SIP Call Flow

2.2.4 WebRTC Session Establishment with Jingle Endpoint

Figure 2.6 shows how WebRTC can interoperate with Jingle. This corresponds to Figure 1.4 and works in a similar way to the mapping described in Section 2.2.2. The media can be directly between the browser and the Jingle client provided the Jingle protocol is extended to support WebRTC SDP extensions, and the Jingle client supports the WebRTC media extensions.

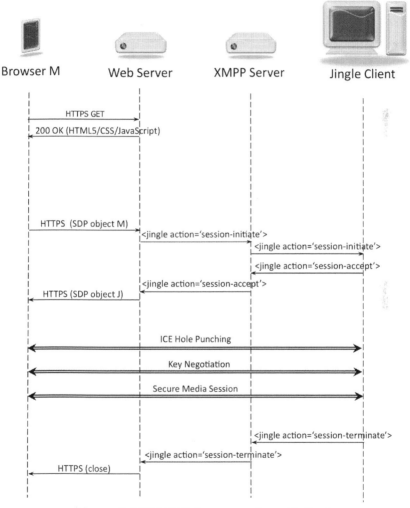

Figure 2.6 WebRTC Interoperating with Jingle

2.2.5 WebRTC Session Establishment with PSTN

Figure 2.7 shows how WebRTC can interoperate with the PSTN. This corresponds to Figure 1.7. The signaling between the Web Server and the PSTN Gateway could utilize any number of signaling or control protocols, or even a SIP trunk [SIP-CONNECT]. The PSTN Gateway terminates the WebRTC media session and connects the audio to a PSTN trunk or line. The G.711 (PCM) codec should be negotiated between the browser and the PSTN Gateway to avoid having to transcode or convert the audio signal.

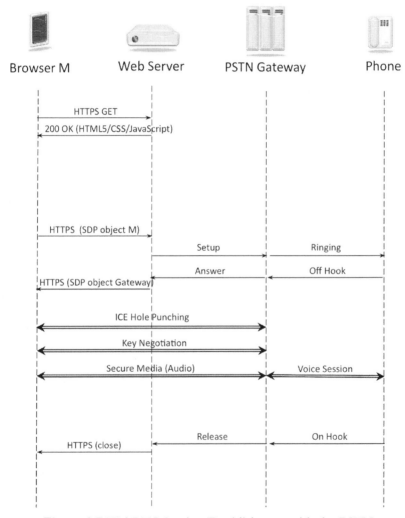

Figure 2.7 WebRTC Session Establishment with the PSTN

2.2.6 WebRTC Session Establishment with SIP and Media Gateway

A slightly different way for WebRTC to interwork with SIP is shown in Figures 2.8 and 2.9. In this example, the media is no longer completely end-to-end. Instead, a Media Gateway is used to terminate the ICE and SRTP, and the media is forwarded to the SIP UA, perhaps even as unencrypted RTP, although this should only be done if the VoIP network utilizes some other security protocol such as IPsec [IPSEC]. This is how VoIP and video endpoints that do not support all the RTP extensions of WebRTC could interwork with WebRTC.

The Media Gateway could also be a border element, known as a Session Border Controller (SBC), used to enable firewall traversal at the edge of a enterprise or service provider network

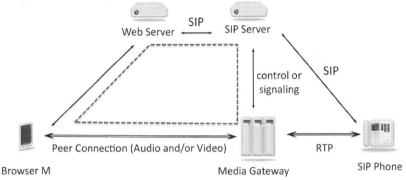

Figure 2.8 WebRTC Alternative SIP Interworking

The details of the messaging between the elements of Figure 2.10 is shown in Figure 2.11.

2.3 WebRTC Pseudo-Code Example

This section contains a simple example corresponding to the media flows in Figures 1.9 and 4.3 through 4.6. The sample code is as close as possible to expected real code use for the WebRTC API; however, it is NOT real code because the APIs are still in flux. Additionally, in some places in the code we provide only comments rather than actual code, either because that code is irrelevant and out of scope for WebRTC, or because it has not been defined yet. For that reason we refer to this as pseudo code. You should in particular be aware of the following: no HTML code is shown, although the outputs (display, speakers, etc.) are assumed to have been set up; the media constraints shown have not been defined, although constraints similar to them are under discussion; and finally, real code would have error handling, but this has none. With these caveats, the remaining text of this section describes the examples.

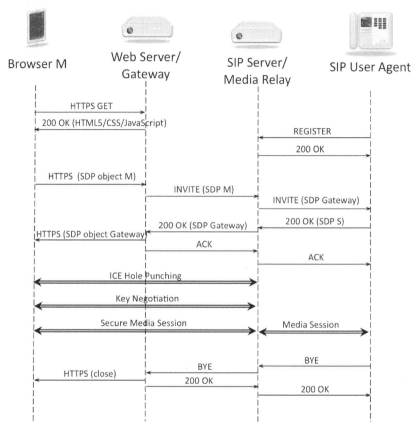

Figure 2.9 Alternative WebRTC Interworking with Media Gateway

The WebRTC specification contains an example in section 7 [EXAMPLE] showing code that is intended to run on both the caller and called sites. For easier understanding, to show different media streams in the two directions, and to show different arrangements of when the local media is obtained, the following example is shown in two separate code segments. The first segment is the code running on the mobile device, and it is hard-coded to place a call (as opposed to receiving one). It obtains local media first, then sets up the connection with the remote peer (laptop). It then creates new media streams from the local ones and attaches them to the new PeerConnection. Finally, it starts the call by creating an SDP offer, notifying the browser of the session description via setLocalDescription(), and sending it to the remote peer.

The second segment is the code running on the laptop, and it is hard-coded to receive a call (as opposed to placing one). Unlike the first code segment, all of the real work of obtaining local media, attaching streams to the peer connection, and creating and sending an SDP answer all take place only after a message is received on the signaling channel. Until then it waits.

Note in this code snippet that the local media is not obtained until *after* the message is received on the signaling channel. If obtaining the user's permission to access the local devices is a slow process, a real-world application might want to obtain the local media in advance of waiting for a call. Notice also that the call to `answer()` is not done until we have actually received the offer from the caller.

ᴊdo Code for Mobile Browser

```
  /////////////
  THIS IS PSEUDO CODE.  Yes, it looks just like real code.
// DON'T BE FOOLED.
// It is pseudo code because the APIs are still changing.
// Don't expect this to run anywhere!
//////////////////

var pc;
var configuration =
  {"iceServers":[{"url":"stun:198.51.100.9"},
                {"url":"turn:198.51.100.2",
                "credential":"myPassword"}]};
var microphone, application, front, rear;
var presentation, presenter, demonstration;
var remote_av, stereo, mono;
var display, left, right;

var signalingChannel = createSignalingChannel();
////////////////////////////////////////////////////////////
// Step zero is to set up the signaling channel.  There is no
// requirement on how this is done.  The identity of the peer
// is determined during the setup of the signaling channel.
// As a result, the RTCPeerConnection itself does not
// have any configuration info indicating the identity of
// the peer. The preliminary code snippets below assume that
// this signaling channel has a send() method and an onmessage
// handler.  The former sends its argument to the peer, where
// it causes the onmessage handler to execute.
////////////////////////////////////////////////////////////

///////////////////////////////////
// These are the three main calls
///////////////////////////////////

// First, obtain local media
getMedia();

// Next, create the peer connection
createPC();

// Attach media to the peer connection
attachMedia();

// Generate and send SDP offer to peer
call();


///////////////////////
// Below this point are the function and handler definitions
///////////////////////

// Get local media
function getMedia() {
    // get local audio (microphone)
    navigator.getUserMedia({"audio": true }, function (stream) {
      microphone = stream;
    });
```

26

```
    // get local video (application sharing)
    ///// This is outside the scope of this specification.
    ///// Assume that 'application' has been set to this stream.
    //

    // get local video (front camera)
    // note that "enumDirection" has not yet been defined as a
    // constraint
    constraint =
      {"video": {"mandatory": {"enumDirection": "front"}}};
    navigator.getUserMedia(constraint, function (stream) {
      front = stream;
    });

    // get local video (rear camera)
    // note that "enumDirection" has not yet been defined as a
    // constraint
    constraint =
      {"video": {"mandatory": {"enumDirection": "rear"}}};
    navigator.getUserMedia(constraint, function (stream) {
      rear = stream;
    });
}

// Create a Peer Connection and set callbacks
function createPC() {
    pc = new RTCPeerConnection(configuration);

    // send any ice candidates to the other peer
    pc.onicecandidate = function (evt) {
        signalingChannel.send(
            JSON.stringify({ "candidate": evt.candidate }));
    };

    // process addition of remote streams
    pc.onaddstream =
      function (evt) {handleIncomingStream(evt.stream);};
}

// attach media to PC
function attachMedia() {
    // Create streams to send
presentation =
      new MediaStream([microphone.audioTracks.item(0),
                       application.videoTracks.item(0)]);
    presentation.audioTracks.item(0).label = "Audio";
    presentation.videoTracks.item(0).label = "Presentation";
    presenter =
      new MediaStream([microphone.audioTracks.item(0),
                       front.videoTracks.item(0)]);
    presenter.audioTracks.item(0).label = "Audio";
    presenter.videoTracks.item(0).label = "Presenter";
    demonstration =
      new MediaStream([microphone.audioTracks.item(0),
                       rear.videoTracks.item(0)]);
    demonstration.audioTracks.item(0).label = "Audio";
    demonstration.videoTracks.item(0).label = "Demonstration";
```

27

```
    // Add streams to Peer Connection
    pc.addStream(presentation);
    pc.addStream(presenter);
    pc.addStream(demonstration);
}


// initiate a call by creating and sending an SDP offer
function call() {
    // Note at this point that we have not yet begun the media
    // offer/answer process, so no media is flowing.

    // Create an SDP offer based on the current set of streams
    // and ICE candidates.  gotDescription() will be called with
    // this offer.
    pc.createOffer(gotDescription);

    // This function acts based on an SDP offer just
    // created by the browser.
    function gotDescription(desc) {
        // First, tell the browser that this SDP offer is my
        // local session description.
        pc.setLocalDescription(desc);

        // Send the offer to the peer as a JSON string
        signalingChannel.send(JSON.stringify({ "sdp": desc }));
    }
}


// do something with remote streams as they appear
function handleIncomingStream(s) {
  // save handles for all incoming streams.  For the
  // av_stream, present it.
  if (s.videoTracks.length == 1) {
    // then this must be the av_stream
    av_stream = s;
    show_av(av_stream);
  } else if (s.audioTracks.length == 2) {
    // then this must be the stereo stream
    stereo = s;
  } else {
    // must be the mono stream
    mono = s;
  }
}


// display/play streams by attaching them to elements
function show_av(s) {
  // display is a video element, while left and right are audio
  // elements
  display.src = URL.createObjectURL(s.videoTracks.item(0));
  left.src = URL.createObjectURL(s.audioTracks.item(0));
  right.src = URL.createObjectURL(s.audioTracks.item(1));
}


// handle incoming messages from the peer.  They will either be
// SDP or they will be ICE candidates.
signalingChannel.onmessage = function (msg) {
    // first parse the JSON event data back into an object
    var signal = JSON.parse(msg.data);
```

```
if (signal.sdp) {
    // If this is SDP from the peer, tell the browser it is
    // the remote's session description.
    pc.setRemoteDescription(
      new RTCSessionDescription(signal.sdp));
} else {
    // If not, this must be a candidate from the peer.  Tell
    // the browser that this is a candidate IP address
    // through which the media could possibly reach the
    //  peer.  The browser will then use ICE to try to reach
    // this address.
    pc.addIceCandidate(
      new RTCIceCandidate(signal.candidate));
}
};
```

2.3.2 Pseudo Code for Laptop Browser

```
////////////////////
//  THIS IS PSEUDO CODE.  Yes, it looks just like real code.
//  DON'T BE FOOLED.
//  It is pseudo code because the APIs are still changing.
//  Don't expect this to run anywhere!
////////////////////

var pc;
var configuration =
  {"iceServers":[{"url":"stun:198.51.100.9"},
                 {"url":"turn:198.51.100.2",
                  "credential":"myPassword"}]};
var webcam, left, right;
var av, stereo, mono;
var presentation, presenter, demonstration;
var speaker, win1, win2, win3;

var signalingChannel = createSignalingChannel();
///////////////////////////////////////////////////////////////
//  Step zero is to set up the signaling channel.  There is no
//  requirement on how this is done.  The identity of the peer
//  is determined during the setup of the signaling channel.
//  As a result, the RTCPeerConnection itself does not
//  have any configuration info indicating the identity of
//  the peer. The preliminary code snippets below assume that
//  this signaling channel has a send() method and an onmessage
//  handler.  The former sends its argument to the peer, where
//  it causes the onmessage handler to execute.
///////////////////////////////////////////////////////////////

// At this end we basically just wait for an SDP offer to come
// our way before we set up the peer connection, obtain local
// media, and attach it.

// There isn't really anything to answer.  This just creates a
// PC and the handlers to deal with incoming streams.  It also
// sets up media.  It is called by the signaling channel's
// onmessage handler.
function prepareForIncomingCall() {
    // First, create the Peer Connection
    createPC();

    // Next, obtain local media
    getMedia();

    // Attach media to the peer connection
    attachMedia();
}

////////////////////
// Below this point are the function and handler definitions
////////////////////

// Create a Peer Connection and set callbacks
function createPC() {
    pc = new RTCPeerConnection(configuration);
```

```
    // send any ice candidates to the other peer
    pc.onicecandidate = function (evt) {
        signalingChannel.send(
            JSON.stringify({ "candidate": evt.candidate }));
    };

    // process addition of remote streams
    pc.onaddstream =
        function (evt) {handleIncomingStream(evt.stream);};
}

// Get local media
function getMedia() {

    // get local video (webcam)
    navigator.getUserMedia({"video": true }, function (stream) {
      webcam = stream;
    });

    // get local audio (left stereo channel)
    // note that "enumDirection" has not yet been defined as
    // a constraint
    constraint =
      {"audio": {"mandatory": {"enumDirection": "left"}}};
    navigator.getUserMedia(constraint, function (stream) {
      left = stream;
    });

    // get local audio (right stereo channel)
    // note that "enumDirection" has not yet been defined as a
    // constraint
    constraint =
      {"audio": {"mandatory": {"enumDirection": "right"}}};
    navigator.getUserMedia(constraint, function (stream) {
      right = stream;
    });
}

// attach media to PC
function attachMedia() {
    // Create streams to send
    av = new MediaStream([webcam.videoTracks.item(0),
                          left.audioTracks.item(0),
                          right.audioTracks.item(0)]);
    av.videoTracks.item(0).label = "Video";
    av.audioTracks.item(0).label = "Left";
    av.audioTracks.item(1).label = "Right";
    stereo = new MediaStream([left.audioTracks.item(0),
                              right.audioTracks.item(0)]);
    stereo.audioTracks.item(0).label = "Left";
    stereo.audioTracks.item(1).label = "Right";
    mono = left;
    mono.audioTracks.item(0).label = "Left";

    // Add streams to Peer Connection
    pc.addStream(av);
    pc.addStream(stereo);
    pc.addStream(mono);
}
```

```
// answer the call by creating and sending an SDP answer
function answer() {
    // Note at this point that we have not begun the media
    // offer/answer process, so no media is flowing.

    // Create an SDP answer based on the remote session
    // description and the current set of streams and ICE
    // candidates. gotDescription() will be called with this
    // answer.
    pc.createAnswer(pc.remoteDescription, gotDescription);

    // This function acts based on an SDP offer just
    // created by the browser.
    function gotDescription(desc) {
        // First, tell the browser that this SDP answer is my
        // local session description.
        pc.setLocalDescription(desc);

        // Send the answer to the peer as a JSON string
        signalingChannel.send(JSON.stringify({ "sdp": desc }));
    }
}

// do something with remote streams as they appear
function handleIncomingStream(s) {
    // take audio from only one stream but display all video
    // tracks
    if (s.videoTracks.item(0).label == "Presentation") {
        // use audio and display presentation screen
        speaker.src = URL.createObjectURL(s.audioTracks.item(0));
        win1.src = URL.createObjectURL(s.videoTracks.item(0));
    } else if (s.videoTracks.item(0).label == "Presenter") {
        // display presenter
        win2.src = URL.createObjectURL(s.videoTracks.item(0));
    } else {
        // must be demonstration, so display it
        win3.src = URL.createObjectURL(s.videoTracks.item(0));
    }
}


// handle incoming messages from the peer.  They will either be
// SDP or they will be ICE candidates.
signalingChannel.onmessage = function (msg) {
    // first create a peer connection to answer the call if not
    // already done
    if (!pc) {
      prepareForIncomingCall();
    }
    // now parse the JSON event data back into an object
    var signal = JSON.parse(msg.data);

    if (signal.sdp) {
        // If this is SDP from the peer, tell the browser it is
        // the remote's session description and send an SDP
        // answer.
        pc.setRemoteDescription(
          new RTCSessionDescription(signal.sdp));
```

```
        answer();
    } else {
        // If not, this must be a candidate from the peer.  Tell
        // the browser that this is a candidate IP address
        // through which the media could possibly reach the
        // peer.  The browser will then use ICE to try to reach
        // this address.
        pc.addIceCandidate(new RTCIceCandidate(signal.candidate));
    }
};
```

2.4 References

[XHR]   http://www.w3.org/TR/XMLHttpRequest

[XEP-0166]   http://xmpp.org/extensions/xep-0166.html

[XEP-0167]   http://xmpp.org/extensions/xep-0167.html

[RFC 3261]   http://tools.ietf.org/html/rfc3261

[SIP-CONNECT]   http://www.sipforum.org/sipconnect

[IPSEC]   http://tools.ietf.org/html/rfc4301

[EXAMPLE]
    http://dev.w3.org/2011/webrtc/editor/webrtc.html#simple-example

3 WEBRTC PEER-TO-PEER MEDIA

WebRTC uses unique peer-to-peer media flows, where voice, video, and data connections are established directly between browsers. Unfortunately, Network Address Translation (NAT) and firewalls make this difficult and require special protocols and procedures to work.

3.1 WebRTC Media Flows

For the media flows between browsers discussed in this chapter, the four browsers in Figure 3.1 will be used as a reference to illustrate the concepts. The mobile and the tablet access the Internet through the home WiFi router. The laptop connects through a WiFi router at a coffee shop. The PC connects to the Internet through a corporate router.

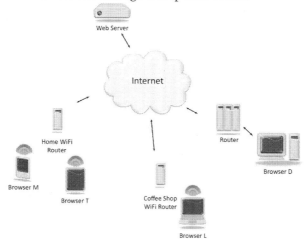

Figure 3.1 WebRTC Browsers Connecting to the Internet

3.1.1 Media Flows without WebRTC

Without WebRTC, it is possible to establish media flows. However, these media flows must follow the same path as the web browsing traffic. In other words, the media packets will flow from one browser to the web server, then to the other browser. This is shown in Figure 3.2 below. The web server needs to handle the extra traffic as a result. High definition video streams can use considerable bandwidth. This limits the scalability of this architecture.

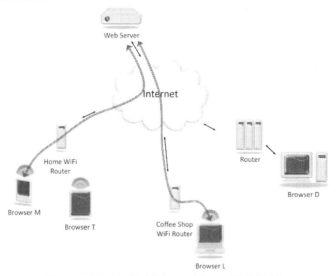

Figure 3.2 Media Flows without WebRTC

3.1.2 Media Flows with WebRTC

The goal of the RTCPeerConnection API in WebRTC is to enable the establishment of direct peer-to-peer media connections between browsers. This flow would look like Figure 3.3.

This path for the media can have few Internet hops, take less time (lower latency), and have a lower chance of packet loss. As a result, these types of peer-to-peer media flows can result in much better quality connections. It reduces the bandwidth used by the web server. It also makes the geographic proximity of the web server to the browsers a non-issue. For example, if the two browsers were located, for instance, in Japan, but the web server was located in Europe, the media flow of Figure 3.2 would be very problematic, but the peer-to-peer flow of Figure 3.3 would be much better.

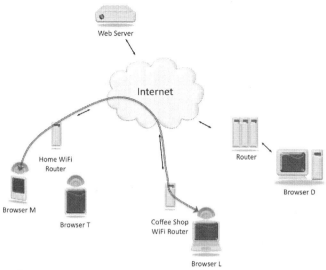

Figure 3.3 Peer-to-Peer Media Flow with WebRTC

However, establishing this media flow is actually quite complicated, as most Internet devices connect to the Internet through a Network Address Translation (NAT) function, as will be discussed in the next section.

3.2 WebRTC and Network Address Translation (NAT)

It is extremely common for browsers to be behind NATs – Network Address Translation devices. A more realistic connection of the browsers is shown in Figure 3.4 with every browser behind a NAT.

NAT is a function often built into Internet routers or hubs that map one IP address space to another space. Usually, NATs are used to allow a number of devices to share an IP address, such as in a residential router or hub. NATs are also used by enterprises or service providers to segment IP networks, simplifying control and administration. Each network behind a NAT is effectively an island, and hosts on that network rely completely on the NAT device providing access.

Many Internet protocols, especially those using TCP transport or a client/server architecture (for instance normal web browsing, email, etc.), have no difficulty traversing NATs. However, peer-to-peer protocols and protocols using UDP transport can have major difficulties. Unfortunately, WebRTC uses both of these.

In Figure 3.4, the laptop is connected to the Internet through a WiFi router that has built in NAT. The mobile browser and tablet browser connect to the Internet through a WiFi hub that has built in NAT and share a single IP address. The PC connects using an enterprise router with NAT.

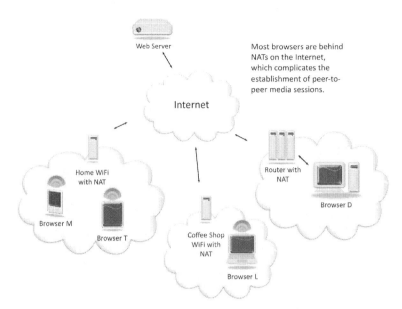

Figure 3.4 WebRTC Browsers Behind NAT

The next sections will discuss the types of media flows that can be established with WebRTC. Some are peer-to-peer across multiple NATs, peer-to-peer behind the same NAT, and relayed through NATs.

3.2.1 Peer-to-Peer Media Flow through Multiple NATs

Figure 3.5 shows a peer to peer media flow that can be established using WebRTC, using the hole punching techniques described in Section 3.3. The media flow can bypass the web server and flow directly between the two browsers, through the NATs.

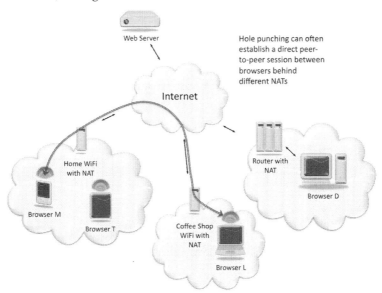

Figure 3.5 Peer-to-Peer Media Flow through NATs with WebRTC

3.2.2 Peer-to-Peer Media Flow through a Common NAT

Figure 3.6 shows the case where a media session is established between two browsers behind the same NAT. In this case, the optimal media path would route through the NAT and never go through the public Internet, as shown. This case also has very desirable quality, bandwidth, and security properties. As in the previous case, hole punching is needed to achieve this media flow.

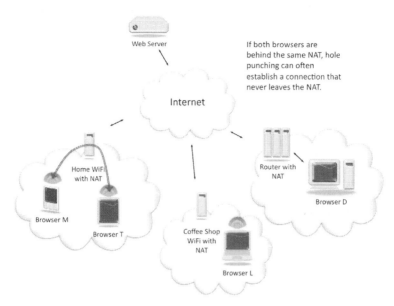

Figure 3.6 Media Flow when Browsers are Behind the Same NAT

3.2.3 Private and Public Addresses

Common NAT terminology uses the terms "private address" and "public address". The IP addresses behind a NAT are "private" IP addresses (used inside each of the NAT clouds in the figures). The IP address (or possibly multiple addresses) assigned to the NAT, and used whenever the NAT forwards packets from the inside to the outside, is the "public" IP addresses. This is shown for the home WiFi network in Figure 3.7.

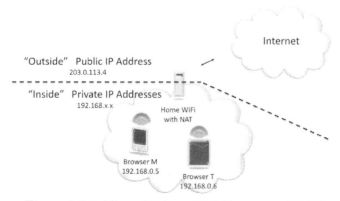

Figure 3.7 Public and Private IP Addresses and NAT

In this example, the home Wifi NAT has been assigned (by the Internet

Service Provider of the house) the IP address 203.0.113.4 – this is the outside public IP address of the NAT, and all hosts that connect to the Internet through this NAT will share this IP address. The mobile device and the tablet each have an IP address that has been assigned by the NAT, which is a private IP address.

Note that these addresses are public in the same sense as we call the telephone network the Public Switched Telephone Network. Public IP addresses are usable (routable) anywhere on the Internet. Public IP addresses have to be unique on the Internet, and they are managed in central registries for the Internet and assigned by Internet Service Providers. They are analogous to a full mailing address including the country name, or a telephone number that includes the country code. Private IP addresses, on the other hand, do not have any special privacy features or capabilities. Rather, they are private as in private property – they are only valid within the network hosted by the NAT. There are specific IP address ranges (e.g. 192.168.x.x, 10.x.x.x, and 172.32.x.x) that anyone may use inside their own network. They do not need to be unique as they are only valid inside that network. They are analogous to a campus box or intra-company mail address, or a telephone number that is an extension, and only valid inside that building or campus.

3.2.4 Privacy

Privacy on the Internet is a very complicated subject, and even privacy in web browsing is also very involved. This book does not discuss topics such as web cookies and browser fingerprinting. There is one aspect of privacy that WebRTC affects which we will discuss here: IP address privacy.

Whenever a browser connects to a web sever, the web server knows the IP address of the browser. In most cases, it is actually just the public IP address of the outer-most NAT that the browser is connecting through. For example, in Figure 3.7, if either the mobile or the tablet access a web page, the web server will get the IP address 203.0.113.4 and not the individual IP address that would distinguish the mobile from the tablet. However, this IP address can reveal a lot about the user, such as location information which is commonly used for location specific ads and search results. There are some services which allow a browser to connect to a server without revealing this information. One such example is The Onion Router [TOR], an anonymizing service for browsing. In general, though, a web server always knows the IP addresses of the browsers that connect to it, and it can do anything with this information including log it, store it, or share it with anyone. For example, there are sites that display this information for troubleshooting purposes [WHATSMYIP] or to correlate anonymous postings. WebRTC does not change any of these well-known web properties.

However, if WebRTC is used to establish direct browser-to-browser media flows, then each browser will learn the IP address of the other browser. This can be true even if the session is not established or is refused by the other party. This information can also include the inside IP address, the private IP address, if this address was shared as a candidate address for hole punching. This is a new privacy exposure introduced by WebRTC and could potentially be used to obtain new information about other users.

If privacy is important in the WebRTC application, there are a number of possible ways to improve the situation:

1) A browser could only send one IP address candidate, that of a TURN server, discussed in Section 3.4. This would allow the other browser to learn where the TURN server is located but not the actual browser using the TURN server.
2) A virtual private network, VPN, service could be used and only the VPN IP address shared as a candidate.
3) A browser might choose not to share the private IP address as a candidate. This would share the public IP address, which might be that of a service provider or enterprise, but not reveal the individual user or computer behind it.
4) A web server could have a policy of intentionally relaying all media traffic, using a TURN server for example. However, users must trust the web site to do this for them.

It is very important to note that in all web browsing cases, some IP address must be shared with both the web server and the other web browser. The only question is which IP address and how much information this reveals about the user.

3.3 Introduction to Hole Punching

The nature of NAT makes establishing direct peer-to-peer sessions difficult. However, using a technique known as "hole punching" [BRYAN], it can be successfully done in many cases, perhaps as much as 85% of the time on average. There are a number of pre-requisites for hole punching. They are:

1) The two browsers trying to establish a direct connection must both send "hole punching" packets at the same time. As a result, they must both be aware of the to-be-established session and know the addresses to which to send the packets.
2) The two browsers need to know as many possible IP addresses as possible that could be used to reach them. These addresses are often described as "private" (or inside the NAT)

addresses, "public" (or on the outside of the NAT) addresses, and relay addresses, depending on privacy settings (see Section 3.2.4)

3) As a last resort, a media relay, which has a public IP address (is not behind a NAT) and hence is reachable by both browsers, is needed.

4) Symmetric flows must be used. That is, UDP traffic must appear to operate in a similar manner to a TCP connection.

Requirement 1) is met by using the Web Server to coordinate the hole punching. That is, the Web Server knows that a session is to be established between the browsers, so it ensures that both browsers begin hole punching at approximately the same time.

Requirement 2) is met by using a STUN (Session Traversal Utilities for NAT) Server, described in Section 5.2.5. Each browser queries the STUN Server by sending a STUN packet. The STUN Server responds indicating the IP address that it observes in the test packet. That is, it responds with the mapped address from the NAT (actually the outermost NAT if there are multiple levels of NAT). This IP address learned from the STUN server is shared with the other browser and becomes a potential "candidate" address. The private IP address is obtained through the operating system from the network interface cards, NICs. These addresses could be IPv4 or IPv6, or a combination of both. This is shown in Figure 3.8.

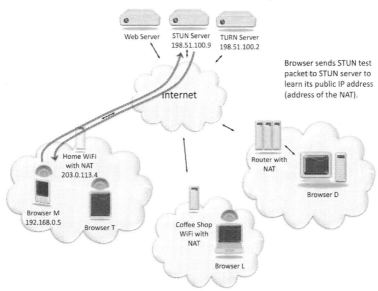

Figure 3.8 Browser use of STUN Server.

Requirement 3) is met using a TURN (Traversal Using Relay around

NAT) Server, described in Section 5.2.6. Just as the browsers query the STUN Server prior to initiating hole punching, the browsers query the TURN Server to obtain a media relay address. This address is then added to the candidate list.

Requirement 4) is met by the browser sending media from the same UDP port that the browser is using to listen for incoming media. This makes the two one-way RTP sessions over UDP appear to the NAT to be one bi-directional RTP session. Symmetric RTP is described in Section 7.3.2.

3.3.1 Relayed Media Through TURN Server

In most cases, the hole punching will result in a direct peer-to-peer connection being established. However, in certain cases of a very restrictive NAT or firewall, the direct paths will fail and the only one that succeeds will be the address of the TURN server. This will result it the media being relayed through the TURN server, as shown in Figure 3.9.

While this is not ideal, at least the media is not being relayed through the Web Server as it was in Figure 3.2. Also, this is only occurring in a limited number of scenarios because there is no alternative – all direct media paths have failed.

The protocol used to implement hole punching, known as ICE, Interactive Connectivity Establishment, is discussed in Section 7.3.1.

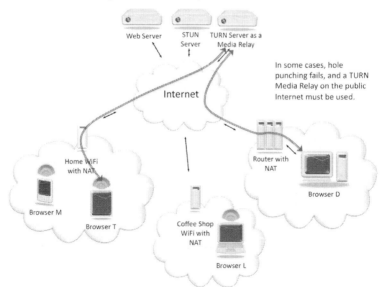

Figure 3.9 Media Relayed Through TURN Server

44

3.4 WebRTC and Firewalls

Firewalls, named after the fire-proof walls used to stop the spread of fires or heat in buildings and cars, are also frequently found in the Internet. They are used at a network boundary to enforce security policies. They can implement any type of policy and do any type of IP packet filtering or blocking. Most commonly, firewalls implement simple packet filter rules similar to those used in NAT. Firewalls act as a "one way gate", allowing access from "inside" the network to the "outside" (the Internet), but blocking arbitrary traffic from the Internet from entering the network. Essentially, firewalls try to allow normal IP traffic originating from inside the network, but block malicious traffic from the Internet.

One type of policy is to allow only outgoing traffic, with the exception of packets from the outside that are determined to be valid responses to requests from the inside. For example, a firewall might allow TCP connections if they are opened from a host inside the network. Once the connection is open, packets can flow in either direction until the connection is closed. TCP connections from the outside will be blocked. Handling of UDP traffic is more difficult since the UDP packets are not part of a connection, and there is no signaling indicating the start and stop of a UDP flow. Outgoing UDP packets might also be allowed, and certain incoming UDP packets if they are destined for a host that recently sent out a UDP packet.

Firewalls are often combined with NAT and implemented in the same box, although they are separate functions. Most home routers and enterprise routers have firewall functionality built in. It is becoming increasingly common for PCs themselves to have firewall functionality, since IP access is handled by the operating system.

3.4.1 WebRTC Firewall Traversal

Hole punching techniques used to traverse NATs often also work for traversal of firewalls. However, some firewalls have stricter rules that cause hole punching to fail. Some firewalls even block all UDP traffic entirely. (For these cases, there have been some discussions of standardizing the transport of SRTP media over HTTP.)

There are a number of different approaches used to help today's VoIP and video traffic traverse firewalls. One approach is to build awareness of the VoIP signaling and media protocols into the firewall, so that it can open "pin holes" for the media only for the duration of the media session. This approach is sometimes known as the Application Layer Gateway or ALG approach. This approach is not usable with WebRTC since there is no standardized signaling protocol used – the signaling is just part of the exchange over HTTP between the browser and the web server.

Another approach uses a special-purpose VoIP and video firewall which is trusted by the firewall. These elements are commonly known as Session Border Controllers or SBCs. They terminate the VoIP and video signaling and media traffic and apply policy. The SBC is connected to the firewall using a trusted link known as a DMZ (for De-Militarized Zone). Again, this approach will not work unless WebRTC is gatewayed to a standard signaling protocol such as SIP.

One approach that could be used is to utilize a media relay which is trusted by the firewall. The media relay would also be connected via the DMZ and would be responsible for authenticating the flows. A TURN Server provides this functionality in a way that is compatible with the ICE hole punching used in WebRTC. Essentially, an enterprise that wanted to be able to control and monitor WebRTC media flows would implement firewall policies that would cause all the hole punching candidates with the exception of the enterprise TURN server to fail. As a result, all flows would be authenticated and relayed by the TURN server. The TURN server could be configured in a web browser in the same way (and for the same reason) as web proxies are configured today.

Alternatively, a firewall could implement an ICE ALG. This would allow the firewall to use the ICE hole punching as signaling for the UDP flows to come. The pinhole could be kept open as long as the ICE keep-alive packets continue.

Figure 3.10 shows media through a firewall using a TURN Server.

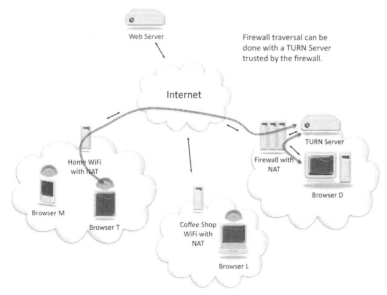

Figure 3.10 Media Relayed through Firewall Traversal TURN Server

3.5 References

[TOR]   http://www.torproject.org

[WHATSMYIP]   http://www.whatismyip.com

[BRYAN]   http://www.brynosaurus.com/pub/net/p2pnat

4 W3C WEBRTC DOCUMENTS

WebRTC is defined by the APIs, many of which are still-being-written. The following sections describe the W3C WebRTC standards documents. Links to both the public working draft and the editor's drafts are provided for reference. Appendix A describes the W3C standards process.

4.1 WebRTC API Reference

Tables 4.1 through 4.6 list the WebRTC APIs and provide a summary of their use. Those documents are described in the next two sections. In the tables, the Reference column (Ref) indicates in which W3C document the API is defined, and contains the value "PC" for Peer Connection [1], described in Section 4.3.1, or "gUM" for getUserMedia [2] described in Section 4.3.2.

Interface and Description	Ref
`AudioMediaStreamTrack` A `MediaStreamTrack` that carries audio and DTMF.	PC
`LocalMediaStream` Represents a media stream local to the current browser.	gUM
`MediaStream` Represents a collection of `MediaStreamTrack`s, currently only audio and video.	gUM
`MediaStreamTrack` Represents a single track of a media source. Note that a track can consist of multiple channels, as with a 6-channel surround sound source encoded into a single track. Also, a track may only contain one kind of media regardless of how many channels it has.	gUM
`MediaStreamTrackList` Represents an ordered list of MediaStreamTracks.	gUM
`NavigatorUserMedia` Pre-existing interface in all web browsers.	gUM
`URL` Pre-existing interface in all web browsers.	gUM
`NavigatorUserMediaError` Represents an error returned from a call to `NavigatorUserMedia.getUserMedia()`.	gUM
`RTCIceCandidate` Container for an ICE candidate.	PC
`RTCPeerConnection` Represents a WebRTC connection between two peers.	PC
`RTCSessionDescription` Container for SDP offer, answer, or pranswer (provisional answer).	PC

Table 4.1 WebRTC API Interface Summary
(PC=Peer Connection [1], gUM=getUserMedia [2])

Constraint and Description	Type	Ref
`MediaStreamConstraints` Contains constraints for selection of audio tracks, video tracks, both, or neither.	Dictionary	gUM
`MediaTrackConstraints` Contains mandatory and/or optional constraints for use when selecting tracks of a single media type (audio or video).	Dictionary	gUM
`MediaTrackConstraintSet` Contains one or more key-value pairs, where each key is a constraint to be satisfied. Used to represent a set of mandatory constraints.	Dictionary	gUM
`MediaTrackConstraint` Contains one key-value pair, where the key is a constraint to be satisfied. Used to represent a single optional constraint.	Dictionary	gUM

Table 4.2 WebRTC Constraint APIs
(PC=Peer Connection [1], gUM=getUserMedia [2])

RTCPeerConnection API and Description	Type	Ref
RTCPeerConnection Represents a WebRTC connection between two peers.	Interface	PC
new RTCPeerConnection(configuration) Creates a new RTCPeerConnection object using the given STUN and TURN server information. The configuration parameter is of type RTCConfiguration.	Constructor	PC
RTCPeerConnection.close() Closes the RTCPeerConnection, effectively removing all attached streams and closing all attached DataChannels.	Method	PC
RTCPeerConnection.createDataChannel() Creates a new DataChannel having the label given as an input parameter.	Method	PC
RTCPeerConnection.ondatachannel User-settable to a function/method that will be called whenever a DataChannel is created.	Attribute	PC
RTCPeerConnection.onopen User-settable to a function/method that will be called when the RTCPeerConnection is first opened.	Attribute	PC
RTCPeerConnection.onnegotiationneeded User-settable to a function/method that will be called whenever local or remote changes to the RTCPeerConnection will result in SDP changes that will require renegotiation.	Attribute	PC
RTCPeerConnection.onstatechange User-settable to a function/method that will be called whenever RTCPeerConnection.readyState changes.	Attribute	PC

RTCPeerConnection API and Description	Type	Ref
RTCPeerConnection.**readyState** Holds the RTCPeerConnection's readiness state: new, opening, active, closing, or closed.	Attribute	PC
RTCPeerConnectionErrorCallback User-settable to a function/method that takes a DOMString of error information as a parameter. Used by RTCPeerConnection.createOffer(), RTCPeerConnection.createAnswer(), RTCPeerConnection.setLocalDescription(), and RTCPeerConnection.setRemoteDescription().	Callback	PC

Table 4.3 WebRTC RTCPeerConnection APIs
(PC=Peer Connection [1], gUM=getUserMedia [2])

SDP Processing APIs and Description	Type	Ref
`RTCSessionDescription` Container for SDP offer, answer, or pranswer (provisional answer).	Interface	PC
`new RTCSessionDescription(descriptionInitDict)` Creates a new `RTCSessionDescription` object. The `descriptionInitDict` parameter is of type `RTCSessionDescriptionInit`.	Constructor	PC
`RTCSessionDescription.`**`type`** Indicates whether the session description is an offer, an answer, or a pranswer.	Attribute	PC
`RTCSessionDescription.`**`sdp`** A string representation of the SDP for the session description.	Attribute	PC
`RTCSessionDescription.`**`DOMString()`** Returns the string representation of the SDP session description.	Method	PC
`RTCSessionDescriptionInit` Container for a session description to initialize an `RTCSessionDescription` object.	Dictionary	PC
`RTCSessionDescriptionInit.`**`type`** Indicates whether the session description is an offer, an answer, or a pranswer.	Attribute	PC
`RTCSessionDescriptionInit.`**`sdp`** A string representation of the SDP for the session description.	Attribute	PC
`RTCSessionDescriptionCallback` User-settable to a function/method that accepts an `RTCSessionDescription` as a parameter. Used by `RTCPeerConnection.createOffer()` and `RTCPeerConnection.createAnswer()`.	Callback	PC

SDP Processing APIs and Description	Type	Ref
`RTCVoidCallback` User-settable to a function/method that takes no parameters. Used by `RTCPeerConnection.setLocalDescription()` and `RTCPeerConnection.setRemoteDescription()`.	Callback	PC
`RTCIceCandidate.`**`sdpMid`** Media stream identifier for the m-line associated with this candidate.	Attribute	PC
`RTCIceCandidate.`**`sdpMLineIndex`** Zero-based index of the m-line associated with this candidate.	Attribute	PC
`RTCPeerConnection.`**`createOffer()`** Creates an `RTCSessionDescription` for an offer with SDP representing the complete set of available local media streams, codec options, ICE candidates, etc.	Method	PC
`RTCPeerConnection.`**`createAnswer()`** Creates an `RTCSessionDescription` for an answer with SDP representing an appropriate set of available local media streams, codec options, ICE candidates, etc.	Method	PC
`RTCPeerConnection.`**`setLocalDescription()`** Records the given `RTCSessionDescription` object as the current local description. If the object is a final answer, media will then change/begin flowing.	Method	PC
`RTCPeerConnection.`**`setRemoteDescription()`** Records the given `RTCSessionDescription` object as the current remote description.	Method	PC
`RTCPeerConnection.`**`localDescription`** The `RTCSessionDescription` representing the currently active local description (SDP).	Attribute	PC
`RTCPeerConnection.`**`remoteDescription`** The `RTCSessionDescription` representing the currently active remote description (SDP).	Attribute	PC

Table 4.4 WebRTC SDP Processing APIs
(PC=Peer Connection [1], gUM=getUserMedia [2])

ICE Processing APIs and Description	Type	Ref
`RTCIceCandidate` Container for an ICE candidate.	Interface	PC
`new RTCIceCandidate(candidateInitDict)` Creates a new `RTCIceCandidate` object from the input parameter. This parameter is of type `RTCIceCandidateInit`.	Constructor	PC
`RTCIceCandidate.`**`candidate`** A string representing the ICE candidate.	Attribute	PC
`RTCIceCandidate.`**`sdpMid`** Media stream identifier for the m-line associated with this candidate.	Attribute	PC
`RTCIceCandidate.`**`sdpMLineIndex`** Zero-based index of the m-line associated with this candidate.	Attribute	PC
`RTCIceCandidate.`**`DOMString()`** Returns the string representation of the ICE candidate.	Method	PC
`RTCIceCandidateInit` Container for an ICE server URL for initializing an `RTCIceCandidate` object.	Dictionary	PC
`RTCIceCandidateInit.`**`candidate`** A string representing the ICE candidate.	Attribute	PC
`RTCIceCandidateInit.`**`sdpMid`** Media stream identifier for the m-line associated with this candidate.	Attribute	PC
`RTCIceCandidateInit.`**`sdpMLineIndex`** Zero-based index of the m-line associated with this candidate.	Attribute	PC
`RTCIceServer` Container for an ICE server URL.	Dictionary	PC

ICE Processing APIs and Description	Type	Ref
`RTCIceServer.`**`url`** A URL of a STUN or TURN server.	Attribute	PC

`RTCIceServer.`**`credential`**
 	
    The credential (e.g., password) to use if the
    `RTCIceServer.url` is the URL of a TURN server.
	Attribute	PC

`RTCConfiguration` Contains an array of ICE server objects.	Dictionary	PC
`RTCConfiguration.`**`iceServers`** An array of `RTCIceServer` objects.	Attribute	PC

`RTCPeerConnection.`**`updateIce()`**
 	
    Causes the browser ICE Agent to restart or update its
    collection of local candidates and remote candidates,
    depending on the parameters given.
	Method	PC

`RTCPeerConnection.`**`addIceCandidate()`** Provides a remote candidate to the browser ICE Agent.	Method	PC

`RTCPeerConnection.`**`iceState`**
 	
    Holds the ICE Agent's current state: `new`, `gathering`,
    `waiting`, `checking`, `connected`, `completed`,
    `failed`, `closed`.
	Attribute	PC

`RTCPeerConnection.`**`onicecandidate`**
 	
    User-settable to a function/method that will be called
    whenever a new ICE candidate is available to be sent to
    the remote peer. This is useful for "trickle ICE."
	Attribute	PC

`RTCPeerConnection.`**`onicechange`**
 	
    User-settable to a function/method that will be called
    whenever `RTCPeerConnection.iceState` changes.
	Attribute	PC

Table 4.5 WebRTC ICE Processing APIs
(PC=Peer Connection [1], gUM=getUserMedia [2])

Stream Processing APIs and Description	Type	Ref
`MediaStream` Represents a collection of `MediaStreamTrack`s, currently only audio and video.	Interface	gUM
`new MediaStream(trackContainers)` Creates a new `MediaStream` consisting of tracks of audio and video from other `MediaStream` objects. The input parameter `trackContainers` is of type `TracksUnionType`, which is an array of `MediaStream`, `MediaStreamTrackList`, and `MediaStreamTrack` types.	Constructor	gUM
`MediaStream.`**`label`** A unique, browser-generated identifier string for this Media Stream defined in the "Media Capture and Streams" document. The "WebRTC 1.0" document explains how remote-originated stream labels are created.	Attribute	gUM and PC
`MediaStream.`**`audioTracks`** A `MediaStreamTrackList` containing all the audio tracks in this MediaStream.	Attribute	gUM
`MediaStream.`**`videoTracks`** A `MediaStreamTrackList` containing all the video tracks in this `MediaStream`.	Attribute	gUM
`MediaStream.`**`ended`** Set by the browser, this attribute has the value `true` if and only if the stream has finished.	Attribute	gUM
`MediaStream.`**`onended`** User-settable to a function/method that will be called when the `MediaStream` finishes.	Attribute	gUM
`LocalMediaStream` Represents a media stream local to the current browser.	Interface	gUM

Stream Processing APIs and Description	Type	Ref
`LocalMediaStream.stop()` Ends all tracks in the `MediaStream`. If there are no other tracks referencing the media source(s), the relevant source(s) is/are stopped and any device-in-use notifications are turned off.	Method	gUM
`URL` Pre-existing interface in all web browsers.	Interface	gUM
`URL.createObjectURL` Creates and returns a "blob" URL for the `MediaStream` given as the parameter. The URL will be suitable for passing to the `<audio>` element if the stream contains audio and for passing to the `<video>` element if the stream contains video.	Method	gUM
`RTCPeerConnection.addStream()` Adds an existing media stream to an `RTCPeerConnection` for sending to the remote peer.	Method	PC
`RTCPeerConnection.removeStream()` Removes one of the `RTCPeerConnection`'s streams from the `RTCPeerConnection`, which will ultimately result in the stream not being sent anymore.	Method	PC
`RTCPeerConnection.localStreams` An array containing all of the locally-originated `MediaStream` values.	Attribute	PC
`RTCPeerConnection.remoteStreams` An array containing all of the remotely-originated `MediaStream` values.	Attribute	PC
`RTCPeerConnection.onaddstream` User-settable to a function/method that will be called whenever a stream is added. This is not yet precisely defined.	Attribute	PC

Stream Processing APIs and Description	Type	Ref
RTCPeerConnection.**onremovestream** User-settable to a function/method that will be called whenever a stream is removed. This is not yet precisely defined.	Attribute	PC
NavigatorUserMedia Pre-existing interface in all web browsers.	Interface	gUM
NavigatorUserMedia.**getUserMedia()** Returns a MediaStream containing one or more media tracks that satisfy the constraints (see MediaStreamConstraints) given as input.	Method	gUM
NavigatorUserMediaSuccessCallback User-settable to a function/method that accepts a MediaStream as a parameter. Used by NavigatorUserMedia.getUserMedia().	Callback	gUM
NavigatorUserMediaError Represents an error returned from a call to NavigatorUserMedia.getUserMedia().	Interface	gUM
NavigatorUserMediaError.**code** The error code that occurred in calling NavigatorUserMedia.getUserMedia().	Attribute	gUM
NavigatorUserMediaError.**PERMISSION_DENIED** A possible value for NavigatorUserMediaError.code indicating that the user denied permission for the page to use the local device(s).	Constant	gUM
NavigatorUserMediaErrorCallback User-settable to a function/method that accepts a NavigatorUserMediaError as a parameter. Used by NavigatorUserMedia.getUserMedia().	Callback	gUM

Table 4.6 WebRTC Stream Processing APIs
(PC=Peer Connection [1], gUM=getUserMedia [2]

Track Processing APIs and Description	Type	Ref
`AudioMediaStreamTrack` A `MediaStreamTrack` that carries audio and telephone events (DTMF).	Interface	PC
`AudioMediaStreamTrack.canInsertDTMF` Indicates whether the track can send telephone events (DTMF).	Attribute	PC
`AudioMediaStreamTrack.insertDTMF()` Sends the given telephone events (DTMF). The duration can be modified.	Method	PC
`MediaStreamTrack` Represents a single track of a media source. Note that a track can consist of multiple channels, as with a 6-channel surround sound source encoded into a single track. Also, a track may only contain one kind of media regardless of how many channels it has.	Interface	gUM
`MediaStreamTrack.kind` Has the value `audio`, `video`, or a user-agent-defined string indicating the kind of media in the track.	Attribute	gUM
`MediaStreamTrack.label` A browser-generated identifier string for this `MediaStreamTrack`. It is optional for the browser to provide anything other than the empty string as the label.	Attribute	gUM
`MediaStreamTrack.enabled` User-settable Boolean to disable and re-enable the output of the track.	Attribute	gUM
`MediaStreamTrack.LIVE` A possible value for `MediaStreamTrack.readyState` that indicates the track is active, i.e., capable of producing output. Note that even if active, the `MediaStreamTrack` may be disabled (see `MediaStreamTrack.enabled`) and thus not producing output.	Constant	gUM

Track Processing APIs and Description	Type	Ref
`MediaStreamTrack.`**`MUTED`** A possible value for `MediaStreamTrack.readyState` that indicates the track has been muted at the source. This can happen, for example, if the user temporarily revokes the user agent's permission to access the source. Note that both audio and video tracks can be muted.	Constant	gUM
`MediaStreamTrack.`**`ENDED`** A possible value for `MediaStreamTrack.readyState` that indicates the track has ended, i.e., that it is no longer capable of producing output and never will be.	Constant	gUM
`MediaStreamTrack.`**`onmute`** User-settable to a function/method that will be called whenever the `MediaStreamTrack` is muted.	Attribute	gUM
`MediaStreamTrack.`**`onunmute`** User-settable to a function/method that will be called whenever the `MediaStreamTrack` is unmuted.	Attribute	gUM
`MediaStreamTrack.`**`onended`** User-settable to a function/method that will be called when the `MediaStream` finishes.	Attribute	gUM
`MediaStreamTrack.`**`readyState`** Indicates the state of the track: `LIVE`, `MUTED`, or `ENDED`. Defined in the "Media Capture and Streams" document. The "WebRTC 1.0" document explains how remote-originated track attributes must be set.	Attribute	gUM and PC
`MediaStreamTrackList` Represents an ordered list of `MediaStreamTrack`s.	Interface	gUM
`MediaStreamTrackList.`**`item()`** Returns the `MediaStreamTrack` at the index given as the parameter.	Method	gUM

Track Processing APIs and Description	Type	Ref
`MediaStreamTrackList.add()` Adds the track given as the parameter to the list if it doesn't already exist, following the rules for track ordering.	Method	gUM
`MediaStreamTrackList.remove()` Removes the track given as the parameter.	Method	gUM
`MediaStreamTrackList.length` The number of tracks in the `MediaStreamTrackList`.	Attribute	gUM
`MediaStreamTrackList.onaddtrack` User-settable to a function/method that will be called whenever a track is added to this	Attribute	gUM
`MediaStreamTrackList.onremovetrack` User-settable to a function/method that will be called whenever a track is removed from this `MediaStreamTrackList`.	Attribute	gUM

Table 4.7 WebRTC Track Processing APIs
(PC=Peer Connection [1], gUM=getUserMedia [2])

4.2 WEBRTC Recommendations

None of the WEBRTC specifications have reached Recommendation status yet.

4.3 WEBRTC Drafts

All the WEBRTC documents are in the Working Draft stage. They are described in the following subsections. Note that the descriptions below are intended to be read in conjunction with the specification documents themselves – they do not repeat everything given in the specifications.

4.3.1 "WebRTC 1.0: Real-time Communication Between Browsers"

This document [1] is the primary document for the WebRTC work, informally known as the Peer Connection draft. It defines the RTCPeerConnection interface, extensions to the MediaStream interface defined in the "Media Capture and Streams" (getusermedia) specification, and an API for communicating data over the Peer Connection channel.

4.3.1.1 RTCPeerConnection Interface

The RTCPeerConnection interface is the primary API of the WebRTC effort. The function of this API is to set up a media connection path between two browsers. Note that the API has undergone a significant change in recent months with the integration of a signaling proposal known as JSEP, the JavaScript Session Establishment Protocol, described in Section 6.3.7. As a result, the specification text is a bit confusing at the moment, particularly with respect to when and how the first MediaStream components are set up.

The constructor for the RTCPeerConnection object takes a configuration object containing the addresses of servers that assist in establishing sessions through NATs and firewalls (STUN and TURN servers, described in Section 5.2.5 and 5.2.6). Optionally, it also takes a MediaConstraints object. The format of this object is described in the section on the "Media Capture and Streams" specification (Section 4.3.2). Currently the specification defines the following constraints: OfferToReceiveVideo, OfferToReceiveAudio, VoiceActivityDetection, and IceTransports. It is important to note that these are constraints on the RTCPeerConnection and not on the selection of media, despite the name of the object.

The RTCPeerConnection object can have associated media streams, of course. These are added and removed using the addStream() and removeStream() methods, respectively. Note that the media streams are not created by these methods; these methods add and remove existing local streams from the set of streams being sent to the remote peer. The localStreams and remoteStreams arrays track the complete set of local and remote streams, respectively. A not very obvious but significant aspect of the Peer Connection API is that it is the responsibility of the web application to manage SDP session negotiation. In other words, addStream() and removeStream() do not cause media to flow or stop flowing. They change the internal state of the local RTCPeerConnection object, but an explicit session negotiation is needed to coordinate the media change with the remote end. To trigger the application code to do the negotiation, the addStream() and removeStream() methods cause a negotiationneeded event to be thrown. When the application catches this event (or sets the onnegotiationneeded callback), the application must then negotiate media by:

1) Calling createOffer() - the user agent will examine the internal state of the Peer Connection and generate an appropriate RTCSessionDescription object (an offer).
2) Calling   setLocalDescription()   with   the RTCSessionDescription object.
3) Sending the generated SDP session description to the remote peer. Note that the specification does not define or mandate the mechanism to send SDP session descriptions to and from the remote peer. The specification occasionally refers to this undefined channel as the "signaling channel".

Of course, if the remote peer were the one to send the offer, the application would need to call createAnswer() instead and send the generated RTCSessionDescription object back. The call to setRemoteDescription() must be done by the application when the remote offer is received on the signaling channel in order for the offer/answer negotiation to be completed. In either case, local or remote, the actual media state change occurs when a final answer is successfully applied in the browser.

An obvious question at this point is why the setup and parsing of the signaling channel, as well as all of the negotiation, were left to the application. The primary reason is flexibility. With respect to signaling, many browser-to-browser communication applications will have both browsers using exactly the same source code from the same web server, making it logical to have the signaling done through the server. Others may want to signal through gateways. With respect to the SDP session negotiation, the two biggest advantages of leaving it to the application are the ability to do "trickle" ICE, where media can begin flowing even before all ICE candidates have been checked, and the ability to modify the SDP if necessary. Since SIP/SDP interoperability is still not at 100%, it is not uncommon to need to adjust the SDP. It is likely that libraries will be developed to support the most common use cases for both signaling and negotiation.

A complexity in the Peer Connection mechanism is that it has two processes, an ICE process and an offer/answer media negotiation process, each of which has its own state machine. The offer/answer state machine is controlled by the JavaScript process, while the ICE state machine is controlled by the browser. The session description reflected in the SDP carries the media offered or answered, as well as the candidates for ICE "hole punching". However, the ICE process is not dependent upon the offer/answer process, which allows for the sometimes slow-moving ICE process to continue checking additional candidates after the media negotiation has completed, i.e., when no more SDP needs to be exchanged in order to agree upon the media. Although in reality there is more than one underlying ICE state machine, since one is needed for each media connection port pair, the WebRTC API exposes a combined state machine. Note that the specification currently defines the following states: `new, gathering, waiting, checking, connected, completed, failed, closed`. There is disagreement and discussion regarding this set, and it is quite possible that the final set of states will differ significantly. However, there is rough agreement on at least having states indicating "collecting candidates", "media can flow now", and "all candidates have been checked".

4.3.1.2 MediaStream Interface Extensions

The WebRTC specification also defines extensions to the `RTCMediaStream` interface defined in the "Media Capture and Streams" specification (Section 4.3.2). First, each `RTCMediaStream` has a `label` attribute to distinguish it from others sent through the `RTCPeerConnection` API. Second, the remote addition or removal of a `MediaStreamTrack` to an existing `MediaStream` will generate local `addtrack` and `removetrack` events. Similarly, remote track muting and unmuting is duplicated locally as well. Third, the specification defines a new `AudioMediaStreamTrack` that is restricted to DTMF (Dual Tone Multi-Frequency) tones and audio samples.

4.3.1.3 DataChannel Interface

The final piece of functionality defined in the WebRTC specification is the `DataChannel` interface, an API for a bi-directional data channel for use over a Peer Connection. In addition to the ubiquitous `label` attribute, the interface also defines a Boolean `reliable` attribute to indicate whether the channel is to use a reliable underlying data transport. This interface is still in flux at the moment. The primary issues are: whether each "data channel" is a separate stream from an SDP perspective, the cost involved in keep-alives for long-lived UDP-based (non reliable) data channels, whether and how much to align the API with the WebSocket API (see Section 5.2.12), and the similarities with and differences from the media API functions.

4.3.2 "Media Capture and Streams"

This document [2] is under the control of the Media Capture Task Force, which is composed of members of both the WEBRTC Working Group and the Device APIs and Policy (DAP) Working Group. Formerly known as the getusermedia draft, it defines the `getUserMedia()` method, the API for requesting and obtaining a local media stream from a device such as a camera or microphone.

4.3.2.1 getUserMedia() method

This API is intended to be the primary API used by all web application developers to obtain access to local device media. As such, it requires the browser to obtain user permission before accessing the device. However, the mechanism for obtaining this permission, the specificity of the permission, the duration of the permission, and all other details regarding permission are left up to the user agent. User agents are encouraged to indicate in a prominent manner when local devices are recording. There are two separate callbacks, `successCallback` and `errorCallback`, for the cases of a successful setup and a failure, respectively. The latter also returns an error code, but at the moment the only valid error defined is the constant `PERMISSION_DENIED`, which has the value 1.

4.3.2.2 Constraints and Capabilities

Although integrated into the specification, the format and processing of the constraints argument to `getUserMedia ()` warrants a separate explanation. This parameter consists of a JavaScript object with one property for each media type (currently only `audio` and `video`). The value for each type can be a Boolean value (explained in a moment) or an object. The object has two optional properties: `mandatory` and `optional`. The former contains a set of constraint keys and values that must be satisfied - if not, an error will be returned. The second contains a priority-ordered list of constraint keys and values that should be satisfied. Failure to satisfy one or more of these optional constraints does not result in an error, but there is a requirement that when conflicting constraints exist, the one occurring earlier in the sequence is to be satisfied. If, instead of an object value, a Boolean value of true is given for a media type, e.g., video:true, then either a video track must be obtained or an error returned. The list of possible constraints is yet to be defined for media.

During the development of this API, some argued for a simpler API that used optional hints rather than constraints, but the constraints approach had two key advantages: an ability for the application to indicate in advance whether certain tracks would be unacceptable, and an ability to indicate whether some constraints were more important than others. For these reasons, and to allow for extensibility going forward, getUserMedia () accepts the constraints parameter described in the preceding paragraph.

The specification will also very shortly define a constraint-based configuration structure, possibly the same as the media constraint structure, and a getCapabilities()method.

4.3.2.3 MediaStream Interface

This document also defines the MediaStream interface, an API for creating objects representing streams of media data. The following subsections describe this interface.

MediaStreamTrack Interface

The foundational unit of the API is a MediaStreamTrack. This track represents the media of a single type that a single device or recording could return. A single stereo source or a 6-channel surround sound audio signal could be treated as a single track, even though both consist of multiple channels of audio. Note that the specification does not define a means to access or manipulate media at the channel level, although it does roughly define channels as having a "well known relationship to each other". From a practical standpoint, the contents of a track are defined in the WebRTC document as "intended to be encoded together for transmission as, for instance, an RTP payload type." In other words, the channels of a track are treated together as a single unit when being transported using a Peer Connection, and even locally with respect to being enabled/disabled or muted.

Interestingly, it is not possible to create a MediaStreamTrack directly; there is no constructor for this object. The creation of tracks will be covered in the following section describing media streams. An interesting aspect of a MediaStreamTrack is that it is essentially just a handle to an underlying browser-managed track (media source). As such, it is possible for a MediaStreamTrack object to become disassociated from its underlying track. Additionally, different `MediaStreamTrack` objects can represent the same media source, which will be explained more fully in the following section describing `MediaStream` objects. Tracks can be disabled/muted individually by setting the track object's `enabled` attribute to `false`. When muted, an audio track will have silence and a video track will show blackness. The `readyState` attribute of a track indicates its status – `LIVE`, `MUTED`, or `ENDED`. Note that a track will also have a status of `MUTED` if the track's underlying media source is temporarily unable to provide media. This can happen, for example, if the end user has suspended permission to use the media source. The state `ENDED` means that the media source is no longer providing and never will provide more media for this particular track.

Creation of Media Streams

A `MediaStream`, then, is a collection of `MediaStreamTrack` objects. There are three ways to create these `MediaStream` objects – by creating a `LocalMediaStream`, by copying tracks from an existing MediaStream, or by receiving a new stream using a Peer Connection. A `LocalMediaStream` represents the original sources and can only be generated by the user agent. Currently the only way to do this is through a `getUserMedia ()` call, although in the future there may be other methods, say, to stream from a local file. One can "copy" the tracks of an existing `MediaStream` object into a new one via the `MediaStream` constructor, which takes as an argument a list of `MediaStream` objects, `MediaStreamTrackList` objects, or `MediaStreamTrack` objects. This is a derived media stream. Note that the elements of the array argument to the `MediaStream` constructor need not all come from the same existing `MediaStream` object; mixing and matching is allowed. Regardless of how the `MediaStream` object is created, a key characteristic is that all of the tracks within the `MediaStream` object will be synchronized when rendered. Tracks are also maintained in a natural order. For example, if two tracks come from a media resource that defines an order among tracks, that order will be maintained. Otherwise, tracks remain in the order in which they are added. Although each track has a label to distinguish it from other tracks in a stream, it is particularly useful for track order to remain consistent when the stream is sent over a Peer Connection. Similar to the `ENDED` status of tracks, a `MediaStream` has a Boolean `ended` attribute indicating whether the `MediaStream` is finished. A `MediaStream` is considered finished if all of its tracks are `ENDED`. Note that tracks in streams constructed from `LocalMediaStream` objects (see next paragraph) are considered to have "weak" references to the underlying media sources, meaning that if all `LocalMediaStream` tracks referencing a particular media source lose their access, e.g., due to the user revoking permissions, then all tracks derived from these, in all `MediaStream` objects, are `ENDED`.

A `LocalMediaStream` has some unique characteristics. Most importantly, the `LocalMediaStream` is tied tightly to user permissions. The user agent is required to obtain/confirm user permission before returning a `LocalMediaStream` (see Figure 6.2). Any user revocation of permission to use a particular media track forcibly sets the status of the `LocalMediaStream` track to `ENDED`. The application may also call `stop()` on the `LocalMediaStream` to indicate that it is finished using the stream, perhaps in response to a user clicking a button or closing a tab.

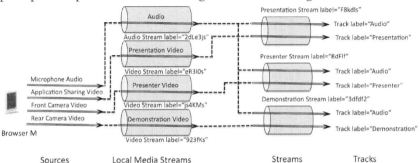

Figure 4.1 Browser M Sending Sources, Streams, and Tracks

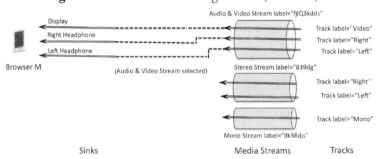

Figure 4.2 Browser M Receiving Tracks, Streams, and Sinks

Media Streams Example

For the media sources of Figure 1.9, one arrangement of tracks and streams is shown in Figures 4.1 through 4.4. In this example, Figures 4.1 and 4.3 show the media flowing from browser M to browser L, and Figures 4.2 and 4.4 show the reverse. The first thing to notice is that the media flow is not symmetrical, with completely different streams flowing in one direction than in the other.

Streams from Browser M to Browser L

Beginning with Figure 4.1, four different media sources are available for use on this device: microphone audio, application sharing video, front camera video, and rear camera video. Through four separate calls to `getUserMedia()`, four separate `LocalMediaStreams` are created. The JavaScript application code then creates three new `MediaStream` objects by mixing and matching. Specifically, the first `MediaStream`, with `label="F8kdls"`, contains a new audio MediaStreamTrack that is linked to the

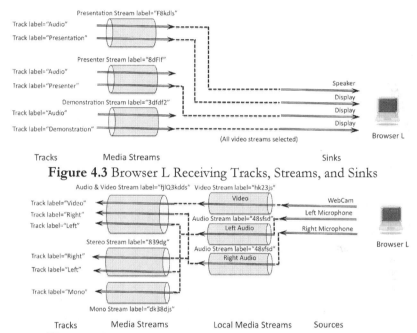

Figure 4.3 Browser L Receiving Tracks, Streams, and Sinks

Figure 4.4 Browser L Sending Sources, Streams, and Tracks

`MediaStreamTrack` in the `LocalMediaStream` with `label="2dLe3js"` (the microphone audio) and a new video `MediaStreamTrack` that is linked to the `MediaStreamTrack` in the `LocalMediaStream` with `label="eR310s"` (the application sharing video). Similarly, the second `MediaStream` contains new `MediaStreamTracks` for the microphone audio and the front camera video derived from the originals in the `LocalMediaStreams`. Finally, the third `MediaStream`, with `label="3dfdf2"`, contains new `MediaStreamTracks` for the microphone audio and the rear camera video derived from the originals in the

`LocalMediaStreams.`

At this point the application code now has four `LocalMediaStream` objects and 3 derived `MediaStream` objects. Notice that the microphone audio track has been duplicated 3 times. The application then decides to send the three derived `MediaStream` objects to the remote peer (on browser L).

Figure 4.3 shows how these streams appear after coming across the Peer Connection from browser M. Notice what the application code on browser L then does with these. It pulls the audio track from the `MediaStream` with `label="F8kdls"` and sends it to the speaker, it pulls the video track from the same `MediaStream` and sends it to one window on the display, it pulls the video track from the `MediaStream` with `label="8dFlf"` and sends it to another window, and it pulls the video track from the final `MediaStream` and sends it to yet another window. Notice that the labels of the received `MediaStream` objects are the same as the labels of the sent `MediaStream` objects. This is how the application can figure out which stream is which!

Streams from Browser L to Browser M

A similar process occurs for the streams originating on browser L that are sent to browser M. In Figure 4.4, on the right-hand side, we can see that there are three media sources being used – a webcam video, a left microphone, and a right microphone. As in the other direction, each is obtained through a separate call to `getUserMedia()` resulting in three separate `LocalMediaStream` objects. These are then mixed into three new derived `MediaStream` objects. The first contains all three tracks, the second contains both audio tracks to make a stereo audio stream, and the third contains only the right audio track to make a mono audio stream. These new `MediaStream` objects are the ones sent over the Peer Connection to browser M.

Figure 4.2 shows how these streams appear after coming across the Peer Connection from browser L. The JavaScript application code in browser M decides to create two new `MediaStreams` – one containing the video from the `MediaStream` with `label="fjlQ3kdds"`, and one containing the audio from one of the three streams, the choice of which is controlled by a button on the display.

4.3.3 "MediaStream Capture Scenarios"

This document [3] is the requirements and use cases document for media capture and media streams. It contains requirements in the following four categories: permissions, local media, remote media, and media capture. The requirements are still under review and will likely soon include requirements from the IETF RTCWEB use cases and requirements draft [draft-ietf-rtcweb-use-cases-and-requirements] document as well.

4.4 Class Diagrams

Figures 4.5 through 4.10 are UML class diagrams as outlined in [4]. Each box shows the class/interface name at the top, the class attributes in the middle, and the methods for the class in the bottom. An empty diamond indicates that the class with the diamond aggregates (collects references to) the class it connects with. A filled diamond indicates that the class with the diamond is composed of items of the class it connects with, meaning that the connected class only exists in conjunction with the filled diamond class. Subclassing is indicated by an arrow, where the subclass points to the superclass.

Diagrams are given for all interfaces defined in [1] and [2]. In addition, custom diagrams are given for all callbacks. Note that the class diagram for `NavigatorUserMedia` in Figure 4.9 only contains the new `getUserMedia()` method.

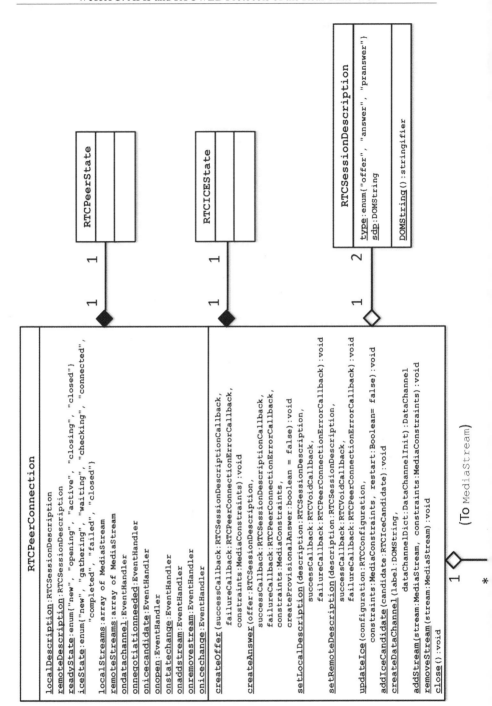

Figure 4.5 Class Diagram for RTCPeerConnection Interface

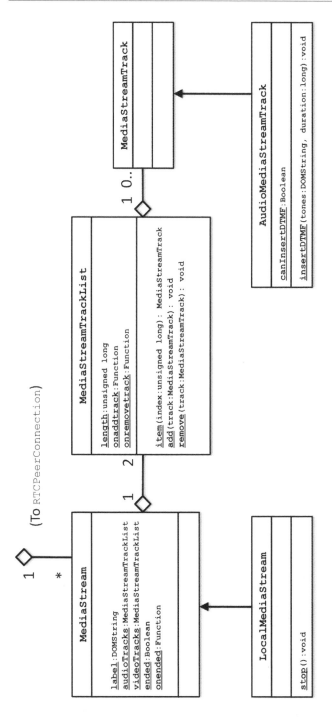

Figure 4.6 Class Diagram for MediaStream Interface

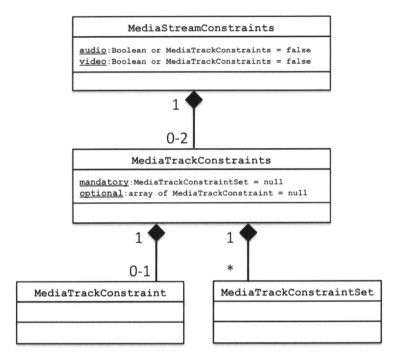

Figure 4.7 Class Diagram for MediaStreamConstraints Interface

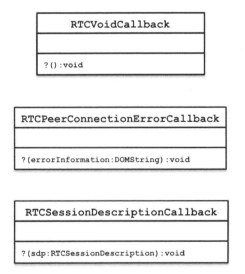

Figure 4.8 Class Diagram for RTCPeerConnection Callbacks

```
NavigatorUserMediaErrorCallback

?(error:NavigatorUserMediaError):void
```

```
NavigatorUserMediaError
code:unsigned short

```

```
NavigatorUserMediaSuccessCallback

?((stream:LocalMediaStream):void
```

```
NavigatorUserMedia

getUserMedia(constraints:MediaStreamConstraints,
            successCallback:NavigatorUserMediaSuccessCallback,
            errorCallback:NavigatorUserMediaErrorCallback):void
```

Figure 4.9 Class Diagram for getUserMedia Interface

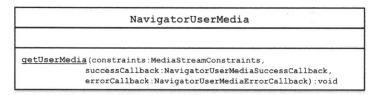

```
URL

createObjectURL(stream:MediaStream):DOMString
```

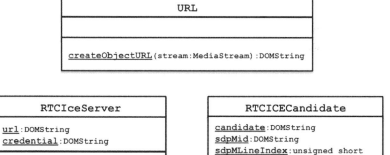

```
RTCIceServer
url:DOMString
credential:DOMString

```

```
RTCICECandidate
candidate:DOMString
sdpMid:DOMString
sdpMLineIndex:unsigned short

DOMString():stringifier
```

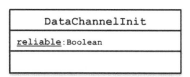

```
DataChannelInit
reliable:Boolean

```

Figure 4.10 Class Diagram for Miscellaneous Interfaces

4.5 Areas of Active Work

There are areas in W3C that are under active discussion but have not yet been included in either an editor's draft or public draft of a specification. For more information on the W3C standards process, see Appendix A.

4.5.1 Statistics API

There is an email thread, with proposal [5], outlining a method `PeerConnection.getStats()` for obtaining statistics on bytes sent and received, packets sent and received, jitter, etc. The current thinking is that stream statistics can be returned for a specific `MediaStreamTrack` or connection statistics for the entire Peer Connection. The interface and set of statistics are both very much in flux at the moment, with outstanding disputes around both the syntax itself and whether statistics on the remote end of `MediaStreamTracks` are also made available.

4.5.2 Capabilities and constraints modification

There are varied opinions on how device capabilities might be returned and how live `MediaStreamTracks` could be adjusted on the fly.

One capabilities proposal [6,7] was proposed at the same time as and is related to the current constraints syntax in the specification. Another proposal [8] suggests significant syntax changes to the existing constraints API in order to enable both a capabilities API and a way to change settings (mistakenly referred to as constraints) of existing tracks. Yet another proposal [9] offers a way to customize live video tracks. There is currently no consensus on either a capabilities API or a way to modify constraints and/or settings of live tracks.

4.5.3 Recording API

There is interest in adding the ability into the "Media Capture and Streams" document to record from a device track. Note that the existing APIs provide a handle to a device track but no access to the content (data) itself. A recording API would change that, allowing the JavaScript code access to the content for saving or additional manipulation. Early email suggestions are expected to be completely rewritten shortly as a new and separable module.

4.5.4 Events

Details are gradually forming in both the WebRTC and "Media Capture and Streams" specifications regarding the specific HTML events that are generated as processing occurs. We expect these details to be complete enough to describe in the next edition of this book.

4.5.5 Risks, Critiques, and Disagreements

There are a few miscellaneous, but important, considerations not discussed elsewhere in this book. Here is a very brief summary:

1) There remain concerns with the use of SDP as the means of representing agreed-upon media flows. While some argue that the browsers will handle all the details, others believe that real-world applications will need to directly modify such representations, both to achieve precise control over behavior and because browser implementations of SDP may vary in their interpretations, and thus behavior. The challenge here is that one of the primary target communities for the WebRTC effort is the web developer community, a group that, generally speaking, will have little or no experience with SDP. This may present a barrier to acceptance by the web developer community.

2) There is a risk that not all of the major web browser vendors will support WebRTC. In particular, Apple (creator of the Safari web browser) has not been very actively involved in the creation of the standard, making it difficult to predict whether or how completely the Safari web browser will support the eventual standard. Microsoft (creator of the Internet Explorer web browser), on the other hand, has expressed continued strong interest in the WebRTC work. However, representatives from Microsoft have conveyed significant concerns with the current direction of the standard, at least partially because of the concerns listed in risk 1) above. It is thus difficult to predict the level of support we will see for the eventual standard in the Internet Explorer web browser.

3) There is continued disagreement about which codecs should be mandatory-to-implement. To guarantee at least basic audio and video interoperability between any pair of compliant browser implementations, the two implementations must support at least one audio codec and one video codec in common. To guarantee this, the working groups are considering mandating support for one or more audio and one or more video codecs. However, the specific choice of codecs is heavily disputed. We will provide more details on this as the various working groups come to better agreement. See Section 6.4.2 for a summary of the codecs under

79

consideration.

4.6 References

[1] Public Working Draft: http://www.w3.org/TR/webrtc, Editors' Draft: http://dev.w3.org/2011/webrtc/editor/webrtc.html

[2] Public Working Draft: http://www.w3.org/TR/getusermedia, Editors' Draft: http://dev.w3.org/2011/webrtc/editor/getusermedia.html

[3] Public Working Draft: http://www.w3.org/TR/capture-scenarios, Editor's Draft: http://dvcs.w3.org/hg/dap/raw-file/tip/media-stream-capture/scenarios.html

[4] http://en.wikipedia.org/wiki/Class_diagram

[5] http://lists.w3.org/Archives/Public/public-webrtc/2012Jun/0239.html

[6] http://lists.w3.org/Archives/Public/public-media-capture/2012Apr/0027.html

[7] http://lists.w3.org/Archives/Public/public-media-capture/2012May/0011.html

[8] http://lists.w3.org/Archives/Public/public-media-capture/2012Aug/0066.html

[9] http://lists.w3.org/Archives/Public/public-media-capture/2012Aug/0032.html

5 WEBRTC PROTOCOLS

There are a number of protocols related to WebRTC. The most important ones are listed in Table 5.1 below. Their usage is discussed in this chapter. They are shown in the protocol stack of Figure 5.1.

Protocol	Use	Specification
HTTP	Hyper-Text Transport Protocol	RFC 2616
SRTP	Secure Real-time Transport Protocol	RFC 3711
SDP	Session Description Protocol	RFC 4566
ICE	Interactive Connectivity Establishment	RFC 5245
STUN	Session Traversal Utilities for NAT	RFC 5389
TURN	Traversal Using Relays around NAT	RFC 5766
TLS	Transport Layer Security	RFC 5246
TCP	Transmission Control Protocol	RFC 793
DTLS	Datagram Transport Layer Security	RFC 4347
UDP	User Datagram Protocol	RFC 768
SCTP	Stream Control Transport Protocol	RFC 2960
IP	Internet Protocol, version 4 and version 6	RFC 791, RFC 2460

Table 5.1 WebRTC Protocols

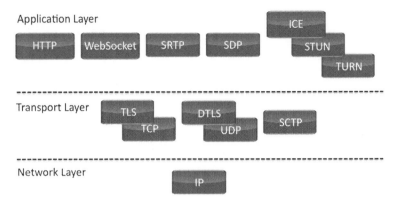

Figure 5.1 Protocols in WebRTC

5.1 Protocols

The preceding sections have discussed the WebRTC APIs as standardized by W3C. Web developers will interact directly with these APIs in their applications and web sites to add communication capabilities. The following sections will discuss the protocols utilized by WebRTC. These protocols are the "bits on the wire" that allow two browsers to communicate, or a browser and a server to communicate. A web developer in general will never directly interact with protocols, as the default settings and configurations of the protocols will usually meet their needs. However, in some cases, especially when a WebRTC client is communicating with a non-WebRTC client, some configuration and knowledge of the protocols used by WebRTC is necessary. Additionally, if there arises a need to adjust the RTCSessionDescription object in the WEBRTC API, such as may occur if there are SDP interoperability problems between user agents, the application author will need to have a deeper understanding of how the negotiation works. In any case, a basic understanding of the protocols used by WebRTC is useful for the developer - this is provided in the first section. A telephony developer who wants to utilize WebRTC, on the other hand, will need to have a detailed understanding of the protocols used. For them, subsequent sections of this book contain a detailed description of how they work together.

5.2 WebRTC Protocol Overview

5.2.1 HTTP (Hyper-Text Transport Protocol)

Of course, WebRTC uses HTTP, Hyper-Text Transport Protocol [RFC 2616]. This is the protocol of the World Wide Web and is used between a web browser and a web server. WebRTC uses HTTP the same as any web application. As such, no specific knowledge of HTTP is needed. The current version of HTTP is 1.1. There is work in the IETF to define the next version of HTTP, known as 2.0. This protocol will likely increase the speed and efficiency of web downloads and applications. WebRTC will be able to use this and any other future version of HTTP.

5.2.2 RTP (Real-time Transport Protocol) and SRTP (Secure RTP)

The most important protocol used by WebRTC is the Real-time Transport Protocol, or RTP [RFC 3550]. WebRTC uses only the secure profile of RTP or Secure RTP, SRTP [RFC 3711]. SRTP is the protocol used to transport and carry the audio and video media packets between WebRTC clients. The media packets contain the digitized audio samples or digitized video frames generated by a microphone or camera or application, and are rendered using a speaker or display. A successful setup of a Peer Connection, along with a complete offer/answer exchange, will result in an SRTP connection being established between the browsers or a browser and a server, and an exchange of media information.

SRTP provides information essential for successfully transporting and rendering media information: the codec (coder/decoder used to sample and compress the audio or video, the source of the media (the synchronization source or SSRC), a timestamp (for correctly timed play-out), sequence number (to detect lost packets), and other information needed for playback. For non-audio or video data, SRTP is not used. Instead, a call to the `DataChannel` API will result in a data channel being opened between the browsers allowing any arbitrarily formatted data to be exchanged.

5.2.3 SDP (Session Description Protocol)

WebRTC session descriptions are described using the Session Description Protocol, SDP [RFC 4566]. An SDP session description (encoded as an `RTCSessionDescription` object) is used to describe the media characteristics of the Peer Connection. There is a long and complicated list of information that must be exchanged between the two ends of the SRTP session so that they can communicate. API calls to `RTCPeerConnection` will result in an SDP session description, a set of data formatted in a particular way, being generated by the browser and accessed using JavaScript by the web application. An application that wants to have tight control over the media may make changes to the session description before sharing it with the other browser. When changes are made to a Peer Connection, this will result in changes to the session description which the two peers will exchange. This is known as an offer/answer exchange (see Section 2.2.1. Any developer wishing to have fine-grained control over the media sessions needs to understand SDP.

Both SRTP and SDP are protocols standardized by the IETF and widely used by Internet Communications devices and services on the Internet, such as Voice over IP (VoIP) phones, clients, and gateways, and video conferencing and collaboration devices. As a result, communication between one of these devices or clients and a WebRTC client is possible. However, few VoIP or video devices or clients today support the full set of capabilities and protocols of WebRTC. These devices will need to be upgraded to support these new protocols, or a gateway function used between the WebRTC client and the VoIP or video client to do the conversion. Telephony and Internet Communication developers can use the descriptions of these protocols in this book to guide their development efforts with WebRTC compatible clients or gateways.

5.2.4 ICE (Interactive Connectivity Establishment)

Another key protocol used in WebRTC is Interactive Communication Establishment, or ICE [RFC 5245] ICE has two important functions:

1) ICE allows WebRTC clients to exchange media across devices that perform Network Address Translation or NAT.
2) ICE provides a verification of communication consent. This means that media packets will only be sent to a browser that is expecting the traffic. A malicious web application might try to trick a browser into sending media to an Internet host that is not a party to communication. This type of attack is known as a Denial of Service or DOS flooding attack. ICE will prevent this from succeeding since media will never be sent unless the ICE exchange completes successfully.

ICE uses a technique known as "hole punching" (see Section 3.3), which was pioneered by online gamers who needed to exchange packets directly between PCs playing multiplayer games despite the presence of NATs between. ICE is run at the start of a session prior to establishing the SRTP session between the browsers. It is also used for the non-media data channel establishment as well.

ICE provides a keep-alive functionality by sending packets at periodic intervals. There is a proposal (see Section 6.5.5) to turn this into a continuing consent functionality by requiring a response and restarting ICE if the response does not come.

5.2.5 STUN (Session Traversal Utilities for NAT)

Session Traversal Utilities for NAT, STUN [RFC 5389], is a protocol used to help with NAT traversal. In WebRTC, a STUN client will be built into the browser user agent, and web servers will run a STUN server. STUN test packets are sent prior to session establishment to allow a browser to learn if it is behind a NAT and to discover the mapped addresses and port. This information is then used to construct candidate addresses in ICE "hole punching". The port number for STUN can be determined using a DNS SRV lookup; the default UDP port for STUN is 3478.

5.2.6 TURN (Traversal Using Relays around NAT)

Traversal Using Relays around NAT, TURN [RFC 5766], is an extension to the STUN protocol that provides a media relay for situations where ICE "hole punching" fails. In WebRTC, the browser user agent will include a TURN client, and a web server, service provider, or enterprise will provide a TURN server. The browser requests a public IP address and port number as a transport relay address from the TURN server. This address is then included as a candidate address in the ICE "hole punching". TURN can also be used for firewall traversal, as described in Section 3.4. The port number for TURN can be determined using a DNS SRV lookup; the default UDP port for TURN is 3478.

5.2.7 TLS (Transport Layer Security)

Transport Layer Security, TLS [RFC 5246], whose older versions were known as Secure Sockets Layer or SSL, is a shim layer between TCP and the application that provides confidentiality and authentication services. Confidentiality is provided by encrypting the "over the wire" packets. Authentication is provided using digital certificates. Secure web browsing today (HTTPS) utilizes only TLS transport. WebRTC can take advantage of TLS for signaling and user interface security. There is also a version of TLS that runs over UDP, called Datagram TLS (DTLS, see Section 5.2.9), and a version that can be used to generate keys for SRTP known as DTLS-SRTP [RFC 5764].

5.2.8 TCP (Transmission Control Protocol)

Transmission Control Protocol, TCP [RFC 793], is a transport layer protocol in the Internet Protocol stack that providers reliable transport with congestion control and flow control. TCP is used to transport web (HTTP) traffic, but is not suitable for carrying real-time communications traffic such as RTP, as retransmissions used to implement reliability introduce unacceptably long delays. Like UDP, TCP uses a concept of ports, a 16-bit integer number, to separate flows and protocols. TCP is provided by the operating system under the browser.

5.2.9 DTLS (Datagram TLS)

Datagram TLS [RFC 6347] is a version of TLS that runs over UDP. The same confidentiality and authentication properties are provided. UDP is easier to get through NAT and can be better suited to peer-to-peer applications.

5.2.10 UDP (User Datagram Protocol)

User Datagram Protocol, UDP [RFC 768], is a transport layer protocol in the Internet Protocol stack that provides an unreliable datagram service for upper layers. UDP is commonly used to transport small, short packet exchanges (for example DNS, Domain Name Service packets) or to transport real-time media such as RTP. UDP provides for very fast and efficient exchange of information; however, users of UDP must deal with possible packet loss. In addition, UDP has no congestion control, so users must be sensitive to packet loss and congestion to avoid overloading Internet connections. Like TCP, UDP uses a concept of ports, a 16-bit integer number, to separate flows and protocols.

Most Internet applications use a reliable transport, such as TCP, Transmission Control Protocol, in which lost packets are automatically retransmitted. Web browsing, email, and streaming audio and video use reliable transport. Received packets are acknowledged, and a lack of an acknowledgement after a certain amount of time triggers a retransmission of the packets until an acknowledgement is received. Real-time communication cannot take advantage of this type of reliable transport due to the time delay involved in detecting packet loss and receiving retransmitted packets. Lost packets in a web page load could result in a page taking an extra second or two to fully load. A real-time communication session cannot pause for a second or two in the middle of a voice conversation, or freeze playing back video for a second while awaiting the retransmission of the missing information. Instead, real-time communications systems just have to do the best they can when information is lost. Techniques to cover up loss or minimize the effects are known as packet loss concealment or PLC.

The average packet loss in general over the Internet is extremely low, on the order of fractions of a percent. Although occurring infrequently, packet loss occurs in a burst, resulting in high packet loss over short intervals. The ability to handle these short-duration loss events has a major impact on the perceived quality of a communication system. Advanced codecs, especially the Opus audio codec (see Section 6.5.8), are designed to provide a good user experience, even during high packet loss. In addition, real-time feedback from the receiver of media also provides the ability to reduce bandwidth or resolution during packet congestion, providing a better user experience and sharing bandwidth fairly with other Internet users.

UDP is provided by the operating system under the browser.

5.2.11 SCTP (Stream Control Transport Protocol)

Stream Control Transport Protocol, SCTP [RFC4960], is a transport layer that provides reliable transport across IP along with congestion control and multiple streams in a session. Congestion control is the ability of a protocol to sense when Internet packet loss and delay is starting to build, and dynamically adjust its sending rate to minimize the effects. Multiple sessions allows a single session to be split into a number of streams, each of which can share the available bandwidth of the session equally.

SCTP is not commonly supported in operating systems, so browsers will have their own SCTP protocol stack built-in for the data channel.

5.2.12 WebSocket Protocol

The WebSocket protocol [RFC 6455] allows a browser to open additional bi-directional TCP connections to a web server. The connection opening is signaled using HTTP and has similar security properties to the HTTP web session, and can reuse existing HTTP infrastructure. This avoids HTTP polling and the opening of multiple HTTP connections between a browser and web server. The browser indicates the application using the WebSocket in the opening. This is known as the WebSocket sub-protocol. The SIP WebSocket sub-protocol [draft-ietf-sipcore-sip-websocket] is an example.

5.2.13 IP (Internet Protocol)

Internet Protocol, IP, is the network layer protocol that underlies the Internet. IP version 4, IPv4 [RFC 791], the current version, is running out of unique address identifiers, known as IP addresses. IP version 6, IPv6 [RFC 2460], was defined to greatly extend the address space to allow the Internet to continue its phenomenal growth into the 21st century. Unfortunately, support and deployment of IPv6 continues to proceed slowly, although many Internet backbones and services and web sites currently support it. Not all Internet Service Providers (ISPs) support it today, unfortunately. Negotiating media and data transport over the different versions of IP can be done using ICE. It is perfectly possible for a dual-stack WebRTC browser to run HTTP over IPv4 and the media over IPv6, or vice versa.

5.3 References

[RFC 2616]   http://tools.ietf.org/html/rfc2616

[RFC 3550]   http://tools.ietf.org/html/rfc3550

[RFC 3711]   http://tools.ietf.org/html/rfc3711

[RFC 4566]   http://tools.ietf.org/html/rfc4566

[RFC 5245]   http://tools.ietf.org/html/rfc5245

[RFC 5389]   http://tools.ietf.org/html/rfc5389

[RFC 5766]   http://tools.ietf.org/html/rfc5766

[RFC 5246]   http://tools.ietf.org/html/rfc5246

[RFC 5764]   http://tools.ietf.org/html/rfc5764

[RFC 793]   http://tools.ietf.org/html/rfc793

[RFC 6347]   http://tools.ietf.org/html/rfc6347

[RFC 768]   http://tools.ietf.org/html/rfc768

[RFC 4960]   http://tools.ietf.org/html/rfc4960

[RFC 6455]   http://tools.ietf.org/html/rfc6455

[draft-ietf-sipcore-sip-websocket]   http://tools.ietf.org/id/draft-ietf-sipcore-sip-websocket

[RFC 791]   http://tools.ietf.org/html/rfc791

[RFC 2460]   http://tools.ietf.org/html/rfc2460

6 IETF WEBRTC DOCUMENTS

There are a number of standards documents that define the protocols used in WebRTC. Some are Internet-Drafts – working documents in the IETF that will continue to be refined and developed before final publication. Others have already been published as RFCs (Request for Comments), the standards documents of the IETF. The draft documents are grouped according to the working group currently discussing and editing each document. Other RFCs that are related to WebRTC such as RTP and SDP are covered in the next chapter.

6.1 Request For Comments

IETF Request For Comments or RFCs are referenced by their RFC number, and do not change with time. There are numerous sources for RFCs including the RFC Editor's Page [RFC-EDITOR]. The RFC links provided in this book are to a conveniently hyperlinked version stored at the IETF website.

Currently, no IETF WebRTC documents have been published as RFCs.

6.2 Internet-Drafts

IETF Internet-Drafts are the work-in-progress documents in the IETF. They change frequently before being finalized as RFCs. Internet-Drafts can be working group documents or individual submissions. Individual documents are likely to undergo the largest changes and will very likely change document names before being published as an RFC. For more information on the IETF standards process, see Appendix B.

6.3 RTCWEB Working Group Internet-Drafts

The main documents of the IETF RTCWEB Working Group are listed in Table 6.1. The relation between the documents is shown in Figure 6.1.

Document	Title	Section
Overview	"Overview: Real Time Protocols for Browser-based Applications"	6.3.1
Use Cases and Requirements	"Web Real-Time Communication Use-cases and Requirements"	6.3.2
RTP Usage	"Web Real-Time Communication (WebRTC): Media Transport and Use of RTP"	6.3.3
Security Architecture	"RTCWEB Security Architecture"	6.3.4
Threat Model	"Security Considerations for RTC-Web"	6.3.5
Data Channel	"RTCWeb Datagram Connection"	6.3.6
JSEP	"JavaScript Session Establishment Protocol"	6.3.7

Table 6.1 IETF RTCWEB Working Group Documents

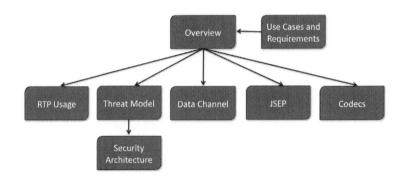

Figure 6.1 IETF WebRTC Standards Documents

6.3.1 "Overview: Real Time Protocols for Brower-based Applications" [draft-ietf-rtcweb-overview]

The Overview working group Internet-Draft [draft-ietf-rtcweb-overview] provides an overview of the protocols and architecture used by WebRTC. The high level goal is to build into a standard HTML5 browser the capabilities for real-time communication with audio, video, and data communications. Codecs for encoding and decoding media streams will be built-in, as will media processing such as echo cancellation (allowing for hands-free or speakerphone operation without a headset or push-to-talk button) and packet loss concealment. A key goal is the establishment of multimedia session between two browsers with the media packets being sent directly between the browsers ("peer-to-peer"). This reduces load, processing, and bandwidth requirements on servers, and minimizes latency (delay) and packet loss on the media path. APIs (Application Programming Interfaces) will be used to expose the browser RTC functions to JavaScript web applications downloaded as part of a web page. This document provides an overall view of the architecture and approach to the WebRTC problem.

This document is currently listed as Standards Track. However, it mainly is a discussion of the WebRTC architecture and philosophy, so it may eventually be published as an Informational RFC.

6.3.2 "Web Real-Time Communication Use-cases and Requirements" [draft-ietf-rtcweb-use-cases-and-requirements]

This working group Internet-Draft [draft-ietf-rtcweb-use-cases-and-requirements] details the requirements and use cases for WebRTC. The requirements include the ability to traverse NAT (Network Address Translation), work with IPv4 and IPv6 and dual stack browsers, utilize wideband and narrowband Internet connections and deal with congestion and packet loss. Use cases include audio and video with multiple sources and streams. Multiparty communication is also described. Applications include conventional telephony calling, meet-me video chat, gaming with peer-to-peer exchange of information, and distributed music making. Interworking with the PSTN (Public Switched Telephone Network) and existing VoIP (Voice over IP) and multimedia systems using SIP and other signaling protocols are also discussed.

This document will be published as an Informational RFC, which will document the thinking and logic behind the design of the actual protocol documents.

6.3.3 "Web Real-Time Communication (WebRTC): Media Transport and Use of RTP" [draft-ietf-rtcweb-rtp-usage]

This working group Internet-Draft [draft-ietf-rtcweb-rtp-usage] describes the usage of Real-time Transport Protocol (RTP) in WebRTC. Browsers will have a full RTP stack built-in as part of the RTC function, as shown in Figure 1.2. The use of the RTP Control Protocol (RTCP) is also specified for the exchange of session information and sender and receiver reports on quality and congestion. Besides the core RTP specification described in Section 5.2.2, WebRTC implements a number of extensions and additions to RTP. Some of these extensions are common, while others are uncommon. This document does not define any new RTP extensions, but references other RFCs and Internet-Drafts that do. The most important difference between regular RTP and RTP as used by WebRTC relates to multiplexing. Normally, each RTP media stream uses a unique UDP port number, and the RTCP session associated with a given RTP stream uses another unique port number. So a multimedia session involving audio and video and associated RTCP sessions would normally require four separate UDP ports. In WebRTC, only one UDP port will be used: all media, voice and video, and the corresponding RTCP sessions will be multiplexed over the same port. This greatly reduces the effort needed to traverse Network Address Translation (NAT) boxes. The details on how to accomplish this are described in Section 6.4.1 and Section 6.5.1. The multiplexing of RTP and RTCP packets on a single port is described in Section 7.1.5.

For backwards compatibility with non-WebRTC endpoints (such as SIP or Jingle clients), browsers will be required to fall back to using multiple UDP ports, as part of normal media negotiation.

A number of conferencing and header extensions are also referenced in this document.

This document will be published as a standards track RFC as it documents the required usage of RTP and RTCP for WebRTC.

6.3.4 "RTCWEB Security Architecture" [draft-ietf-rtcweb-security-arch]

This working group Internet-Draft [draft-ietf-rtcweb-security-arch] describes the security architecture for WebRTC. The basic security model of web browsing is applied to real-time communications. In its simplest form, the human user must trust their web browser. The user relies on their web browser to protect them against potentially malicious sites they might visit. Before a site is given access to a microphone or camera, the browser must get permission from the user. Figure 6.2 shows an example of an actual WebRTC browser (Google Chrome Canary on Mac OS) requesting user consent when a WebRTC application (Meetecho collaboration [MEETECHO]) requesting permission from the user to use the microphone and camera. The permission request is located under the URL bar.

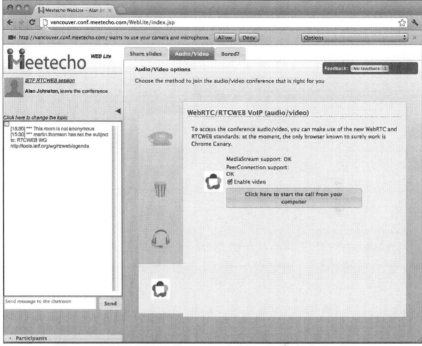

Figure 6.2 WebRTC Browser Asking Permission of User

In addition, the fact that a microphone or camera is being used by a web site must also be indicated to the user. This is shown in Figure 6.3. for the Meetecho WebRTC application.

The document also discusses the ways in which protocols such as TLS (Section 5.2.7), SRTP (Section 5.2.2), and DTLS-SRTP [RFC 5764] can be used to provide security in WebRTC. For example, the use of security provided by HTTPS is discussed, as shown in Figure 6.4.

The use of an Identity Proxy, detailed in an individual Internet-Draft, is also discussed, although this work does not yet have working group consensus.

Figure 6.3 WebRTC Browser Providing Indication to User that Microphone and Camera are in Use

HTML/CSS/JavaScript

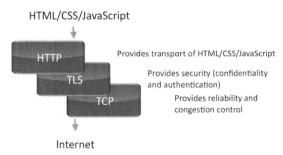

Provides transport of HTML/CSS/JavaScript

Provides security (confidentiality and authentication)

Provides reliability and congestion control

Internet

Figure 6.4 HTTPS Security Layers in WebRTC

6.3.5 "Security Considerations for RTC-Web" [draft-ietf-rtcweb-security]

This working group Internet-Draft [draft-ietf-rtcweb-security] describes the threat model for WebRTC in support of the RTCWEB Security Architecture document. This threat model will be used to evaluate the security mechanisms in the protocol specifications.

6.3.6 "RTCWeb Datagram Connection" [draft-ietf-rtcweb-data-channel]

This working group Internet-Draft [draft-ietf-rtcweb-data-channel] discusses the requirements and protocols used for non-RTP, non-media data exchanged between browsers. The proposal is to use Stream Control Transport Protocol, SCTP (see Section 5.2.11) over Datagram Transport Layer Protocol, DTLS (see Section 5.2.9), over User Datagram Protocol (UDP) as shown in Figure 6.5. This somewhat complicated protocol stack is designed to provide NAT traversal, authentication, confidentiality, and reliable transport of multiple streams. While SCTP is a transport layer protocol, it cannot be used directly on top of IP (Internet Protocol) due to the presence of NAT. Instead, the whole stack is tunneled over UDP so that NAT will not drop packets. ICE is used to establish the data channel to provide communication consent and hole punching to enable NAT and firewall traversal. Note that SCTP will be implemented in the browser itself (so called "user-land") as opposed to relying on an operating system (kernel) implementation.

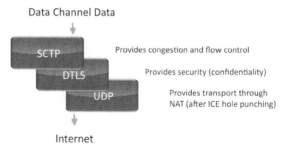

Figure 6.5 Protocol Layers of the WebRTC Datagram Connection

6.3.7 "JavaScript Session Establishment Protocol" [draft-ietf-rtcweb-jsep]

The JavaScript Session Establishment Protocol (JSEP) [draft-ietf-rtcweb-jsep] is a new 'signaling protocol' developed for WebRTC. It is not really a signaling protocol in the way that SIP and Jingle are signaling protocols. Instead, JSEP describes how a JavaScript application running on a browser interacts with the built-in RTC function. It defines how the JavaScript can get information about the capabilities of the browser, including supported media types and codecs – the SDP RTCSessionDescription object. It also describes how JavaScript can manage the offer/answer negotiation of media between the browsers, and the ICE hole punching process running in the browser. It is very important to note that JSEP does not define any on-the-wire protocol – how the SDP objects are sent to and from the web server is not described. (This is expected to be done using a standard web approach such as XHD).

Those experienced with signaling protocols may wonder where the 'state machine' is located. The state machine in WebRTC is not standardized, but is instead just part of the JavaScript code that uses JSEP.

APIs are used to get candidate and capability information from the browser. The ICE state machine runs natively in the browser, and is decoupled from the JSEP state machine. The division of state between the browser and the server is shown in Figure 6.6.

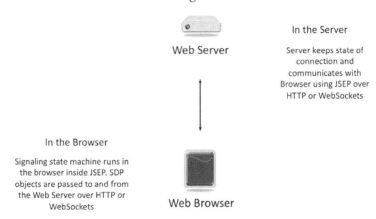

In the Server

Web Server

Server keeps state of connection and communicates with Browser using JSEP over HTTP or WebSockets

In the Browser

Signaling state machine runs in the browser inside JSEP. SDP objects are passed to and from the Web Server over HTTP or WebSockets

Web Browser

Figure 6.6 Division of State Between Browser and Server

JSEP currently uses SDP session descriptions, Section 5.2.3, as the syntax for offers and answers, although a JavaScript Object Notation (JSON) format could be defined in the future. Within the application JavaScript code, some form of an offer/answer state machine is needed. Some initial work was to use the existing SIP offer/answer model, defined in [RFC 3264], but with a different encoding. (This was known as ROAP, RTCWEB Offer Answer Protocol, and was described in a number of individual Internet-Drafts.) However, this was viewed as too restrictive, and this current proposal tries to relax the offer/answer requirements as much as possible. In addition, this proposal tries to deal with the "refresh" or "rehydration" problem where a user manually reloads a web page during an RTC session, although this is still under discussion in the working group. This book does not cover the details of SDP offer/answer. To understand SDP offer/answer, see [SDP-OA].

JSEP will eventually be published as a standards track RFC, although some of the current text in the document may be moved to the W3C WebRTC specification.

6.4 Individual Internet-Drafts

These documents have not yet been adopted as working group items but have had discussion and seem to have some level of support and interest in the IETF.

6.4.1 "Multiplexing Multiple Media Types In a Single Real-Time Transport Protocol (RTP) Session" [draft-lennox-rtcweb-rtp-media-type-mux]

This individual Internet-Draft [draft-lennox-rtcweb-rtp-media-type-mux] discusses the RTP issues associated with multiplexing different media types (e.g. audio and video) over the same ports. When multiple RTP streams are multiplexed, payload types and SSRCs must not overlap across all the media streams. The SDP issues with multiplexing are discussed in [draft-ietf-mmusic-sdp-bundle-negotiation].

6.4.2 "WebRTC Codec and Media Processing Requirements" [draft-cbran-rtcweb-codec]

This individual Internet-Draft [draft-cbran-rtcweb-codec] discusses requirements for codecs and media processing. For example the Opus codec [draft-ietf-codec-opus] is the default audio codec between browsers, with PCM u-law/A-law (G.711) [RFC 3551] and telephone events [RFC 4733] (for DTMF – dual tone multi frequency) for interoperation with the PSTN and SIP and Jingle clients. The default video codec is currently under discussion with H.264 [H.264], VP8 [VP8], and others being considered by the working group. The recommended audio level is also discussed. Requirements for both near-end and far-end echo cancellation are also discussed.

Codec information is summarized in Table 6.2.

Codec	Use	Specification
Opus	Narrowband to wideband Internet audio codec for speech and music	draft-ietf-codec-opus
G.711	PCM audio encoding for PSTN interworking and backwards compatibility with VoIP systems	RFC 3551
Telephone Events	Transport of Dual Tone Multi Frequency (DTMF) tones	RFC 4733
H.264	Video codec requiring licensing	RFC 6184
VP8	Open source video codec	RFC 6386

Table 6.2 WebRTC Codec Summary

6.4.3 "Cross Stream Identification in the Session Description Protocol" [draft-alvestrand-rtcweb-msid]

This individual Internet-Draft document [draft-alvestrand-rtcweb-msid] defines the `msid` attribute extension to the `a=ssrc` source specific attribute extension (see Section 7.2.3). This extension is used to associate a `MediaStream` to an SSRC. As discussed in the WebRTC (Peer Connection) draft, a `MediaStream` is made up of multiple `MediaStreamTracks`. An example of this is shown in the example SDP of Section 7.2.1. More work is needed to finalize this extension.

6.4.4 "IANA Registry for RTCWeb Media Constraints" [draft-burnett-rtcweb-constraints-registry]

This individual Internet-Draft [draft-burnett-rtcweb-constraints-registry] defines an Internet Assigned Numbers Authority (IANA) registry to track all media constraints and capabilities used in both the `RTCPeerConnection` and `getUserMedia` interfaces.

6.4.5 "A Google Congestion Control for Real-Time Communication on the World Wide Web" [draft-alvestrand-rtcweb-congestion]

This individual Internet-Draft [draft-alvestrand-rtcweb-congestion] describes Google's current implementation of congestion control used in their WebRTC open source project.

Congestion control is about the behavior of protocols and applications when packet loss occurs on the Internet. TCP has very advanced congestion control algorithms that have been developed over many decades of Internet experience. In very simple terms, TCP slowly ramps up its throughput. When packet loss occurs, TCP reduces its throughput and backs off, and slowly ramps up again. This allows a number of different TCP flows to share available bandwidth. UDP does not have any built-in congestion control, and WebRTC media flows utilize UDP transport.

This has not really been much of a problem so far in Internet Communication for two reasons. First, these deployments have mainly been VoIP, where the audio bandwidth is quite small. Also, most VoIP systems have used fixed-rate telephony codecs which cannot adapt even if they are aware of congestion.

WebRTC is likely to see a significant deployment of high definition video communications, which uses a significant bandwidth and is also bursty (due to being a mixture of infrequent but large I-frames or key frames, with more frequent smaller P-frames and B-frames). In addition, WebRTC uses Internet codecs such as Opus that can operate over a wide range of bandwidth and can adapt without signaling. The main feedback mechanism is RTCP messages received from the remote peer giving information about packet loss, delay, and delay variation.

There is significant work in the IETF to develop new congestion control algorithms suitable for RTP over UDP flows. These algorithms will use network statistics derived from the RTCP feedback to estimate conditions and detect congestion before packet loss occurs. This information will then be used to rate-limit the bandwidth used by the SRTP media flows and the data channel flows.

The approach described in this Internet-Draft uses RTCP feedback based on Temporary Maximum Media Stream Bit Rate Request (TMMBR, pronounced "timber", described in Section 7.1.11) . The approach uses signal processing to detect congestion before packet loss occurs. The approach uses the TCP Friendly Rate Control (TFRC) described in Section 7.1.12.

The IETF will attempt to standardize a congestion control algorithm for RTP in the future suitable for use in WebRTC browsers. In July 2012, the Internet Architecture Board (IAB) held a workshop on "Congestion Control for Interactive Real-Time Communication". Information about the workshop including a link to the papers discussed is available on the IAB website [IAB-CCIRTC]. At the IETF-84 meeting in Vancouver, BC, Canada in August 2012, an RTP Congestion Control BOF (Birds of a Feather) session was held. Presentations and minutes are included in the Proceedings for IETF-84 [IETF-84].

6.5 RTCWEB Documents in Other Working Groups

Some of the protocols being developed for use in WebRTC are being worked on in working groups other than RTCWEB, as discussed in Section

B.3. The Internet-Drafts are listed in this section.

6.5.1 "Multiplexing Negotiation Using Session Description Protocol (SDP) Port Numbers" [draft-ietf-mmusic-sdp-bundle-negotiation]

This MMUSIC Working Group Internet-Draft [draft-ietf-mmusic-sdp-bundle-negotiation], discussed in the MMUSIC Working Group, defines a new SDP grouping framework extension called BUNDLE (a=group:BUNDLE). SDP grouping is discussed in Section 7.2.4. This grouping allows the grouped m= media lines to share the same port number. WebRTC will use this to signal the multiplexing of multiple media types on the same ports, as described in Section 6.4.1. Backwards compatibility has not been fully designed yet, so this mechanism may change.

6.5.2 "Mechanisms for Media Source Selection in the Session Description Protocol (SDP)" [draft-lennox-mmusic-sdp-source-selection]

This individual Internet-Draft [draft-lennox-mmusic-sdp-source-selection] extends the Source Specific Media Attributes described in Section 7.2.3 to allow selection of a media stream by source. The a=remote-ssrc SDP attribute is used to select a particular stream and set a particular attribute. This specification also defines a number of media attributes that can be set using this mechanism, including recv, framerate, imageattr, and priority. The recv attribute is used to enable (recv:on) or disable (recv:off) a source. If the recv attribute is not present, then recv:on is assumed. The framerate attribute is used to request a particular frame rate for a video stream. The imageattr attribute is used to set image resolution of a media source. The priority attribute is used to set the relative priory among the media sources. If bandwidth or other limitations prevent receiving all the requested sources, the priority is used to decide which sources should be omitted or scaled back.

This specification also defines two new parameters to be used for Source Specific Media attributes: information and sending. The information attribute is used to provide human readable text about a media source, in a similar way to the i= field in SDP. The sending attribute indicates the sending state of a particular source, either on or off. A source may be off due to it being disabled by the receiver, or the sender may just no longer wish to send the source.

In offer/answer SDP exchanges, all parties should list all available sources. Note that sources can be discovered via other mechanisms such as receipt of SSRC in RTP or through other conferencing notifications.

6.5.3 "The WebSocket Protocol as a Transport for the Session Initiation Protocol (SIP)" [draft-ietf-sipcore-sip-websocket]

This SIPCORE Working Group Internet-Draft [draft-ietf-sipcore-sip-websocket] defines a WebSocket transport for SIP. WebSocket, described in Section 5.2.12, allows a Web browser to open a new connection to the web server. While this specification is not required for WebRTC, it is related in that it allows Session Initiation Protocol (SIP) to be used as the signaling protocol. The SIP User Agent (UA) stack would be written, for example, in JavaScript and downloaded by the web server. The SIP UA would then use WebSockets to open a new connection to the SIP Proxy Server. The media from the SIP signaling would use the normal WebRTC methods, e.g. a Peer Connection to establish media sessions. This specification defines a new Via transport token WS (WebSocket) and new SIP URI transport parameters ws (WebSocket) and wss (Secure WebSocket) which uses TLS transport.

Note that SIP signaling between Web Servers, as shown in the WebRTC Trapezoid of Figure 1.4, would most likely not use WebSocket transport, and instead would use normal SIP transport such as TCP or UDP.

6.5.4 "Encryption of Header Extensions in the Secure Real-Time Transport Protocol (SRTP)" [draft-ietf-avtcore-srtp-encrypted-header-ext]

Normal SRTP, described in Section 5.2.2, does not encrypt RTP header extensions, although header extensions are authenticated. This AVTCORE Working Group Internet-Draft [draft-ietf-avtcore-srtp-encrypted-header-ext] defines how to encrypt RTP header extensions. If RTP header extensions, such as those in Section 7.1.6 and Section 7.1.7, are used in WebRTC and need privacy, then this extension may be used by WebRTC. Encryption of the RTP header is specified using the a=extmap SDP extension described in Section 7.1.14.

6.5.5 "STUN Usage for Consent Freshness and Session Liveness" [draft-muthu-behave-consent-freshness]

This individual Internet-Draft [draft-muthu-behave-consent-freshness] discusses some important potential changes to the way in which a browser determines if a multimedia session is still alive, and if the other party wishes to continue to receive the negotiated media. The document proposes some extensions to ICE to add this functionality to ICE keep-alives. This work is being discussed in both the BEHAVE Working Group (which works on NAT issues) and in the RTCWEB Working Group.

6.5.6 "Guidelines for using the Multiplexing Features of RTP" [draft-westerlund-avtcore-multiplex-architecture]

This individual Internet-Draft [draft-westerlund-avtcore-multipolex-architecture] explains how RTP can be multiplexed, the issues discussed in RFC 3550 against multiplexing, and possible approaches to overcome them. It is being discussed in both the AVTCORE Working Group and the RTCWEB Working Group.

6.5.7 "Multiple RTP Sessions on a Single Lower-Layer Transport" [draft-westerlund-avtcore-transport-multiplexing]

This individual Internet-Draft [draft-westerlund-avtcore-transport-multiplexing] defines a shim layer ("wedged" between two layers) for multiplexing multiple RTP sessions on the same transport address. A one (or possibly four) octet Session ID is inserted (shimmed) between the transport header (UDP) and the start of the SRTP header. Unfortunately, this makes the on-the-wire format incompatible with RTP, and it is virtually a new protocol. The Session ID is signaled in SDP using an a=session-mux-id attribute and a=group:SHIM attribute. An alternative approach using the RTP SSRC to demultiplex multiple streams is also under consideration in WebRTC. So far, no clear consensus has emerged in the working group. This draft is being discussed in both the AVTCORE Working Group and the RTCWEB Working Group.

6.5.8 "Definition of the Opus Audio Codec" [draft-ietf-codec-opus]

The Opus [draft-ietf-codec-opus] CODEC Working Group Internet-Draft defines the Internet low latency codec for audio and music known as Opus. Opus incorporates elements and technology from Skype's SILK [SILK] codec and the open source CELT (Constrained Energy Lapped Transform) [CELT] codec. Opus is extremely flexible, supporting bit rates from 6 – 510 kb/s, constant or variable bit rate, sampling rates from 8 – 48 kHz, support for speech and music, mono and stereo, frame sizes from 2.5ms to 60ms, and floating point or fixed-point implementation. Opus also has very good packet loss concealment (PLC) and good quality even during packet loss. The RTP payload for Opus is defined in [draft-spittka-payload-rtp-opus].

This document has been approved by the IESG and is in the RFC Editor's queue, awaiting editing and assignment of an RFC number late in 2012.

6.5.9 "Random algorithm for RTP CNAME generation" [draft-rescorla-random-cname]

This individual Internet-Draft [draft-rescorla-random-cname] defines a new algorithm for generating random CNAMEs, canonical names which are sent over RTCP and used to identify RTP endpoints in a RTP session. This is important for media privacy in WebRTC where CNAMEs could be used to identify senders across sessions and across applications.

6.5.10 "RTP Congestion Control: Circuit Breakers for Unicast Sessions" [draft-perkins-avtcore-rtp-circuit-breakers]

This individual Internet-Draft [draft-perkins-avtcore-rtp-circuit-breakers] discusses the congestion conditions under which RTP senders should stop sending to avoid making congestion worse. This protection is analogous to the use of circuit breakers to interrupt the flow of excessive current in an electrical circuit. WebRTC will also eventually have congestion control algorithms to reduce traffic before this condition is reached.

6.5.11 "Support for Multiple Clock Rates in an RTP Session" [draft-ietf-avtext-multiple-clock-rates]

This AVTEXT Working Group Internet-Draft [draft-ietf-avtext-multiple-clock-rates] provides guidance in the event that the clock rate changes for an SSRC in a media session. This could happen in WebRTC when switching between Opus and PCM codecs, for example, which use different clock rates.

6.6 References

[RFC-EDITOR]   http://www.rfc-editor.org

[draft-ietf-rtcweb-overview]   http://tools.ietf.org/html/draft-ietf-rtcweb-overview

[draft-ietf-rtcweb-use-cases-and-requirements]
    http://tools.ietf.org/html/draft-ietf-rtcweb-use-cases-and-requirements

[draft-ietf-rtcweb-rtp-usage]   http://tools.ietf.org/html/draft-ietf-rtcweb-rtp-usage

[draft-ietf-rtcweb-security-arch]   http://tools.ietf.org/html/draft-ietf-rtcweb-security-arch

[MEETECHO]   http://www.meetecho.com

[RFC 5764]   http://tools.ietf.org/html/rfc5764

[draft-ietf-rtcweb-security]   http://tools.ietf.org/html/draft-ietf-rtcweb-security

[draft-ietf-rtcweb-data-channel]   http://tools.ietf.org/html/draft-ietf-rtcweb-data-channel

[draft-ietf-rtcweb-jsep]   http://tools.ietf.org/html/draft-ietf-rtcweb-jsep

[RFC 3264]   http://tools.ietf.org/html/rfc3264

[SDP-OA]   Chapter 13 of SIP: Understanding the Session Initiation Protocol, 3rd Edition.

[draft-lennox-rtcweb-rtp-media-type-mux]
     http://tools.ietf.org/html/draft-lennox-rtcweb-rtp-media-type-mux

[draft-cbran-rtcweb-codec]   http://tools.ietf.org/html/draft-cbran-rtcweb-codec

[draft-ietf-codec-opus]   http://tools.ietf.org/html/draft-ietf-codec-opus

[RFC 3551]   http://tools.ietf.org/html/rfc3551

[RFC 4733]   http://tools.ietf.org/html/rfc4733

[H.264]   http://www.itu.int/rec/T-REC-H.264

[VP8]   http://tools.ietf.org/html/rfc6386 Note that although this is an RFC, it is not an IETF document, instead it is an Independent Stream Submission

[draft-alvestrand-rtcweb-msid]   http://tools.ietf.org/html/draft-alvestrand-rtcweb-msid

[draft-burnett-rtcweb-constraints-registry]
     http://tools.ietf.org/html/draft-burnett-rtcweb-constraints-registry

[draft-alvestrand-rtcweb-congestion]   http://tools.ietf.org/html/draft-alvestrand-rtcweb-congestion

[IAB-CCIRTC]   http://www.iab.org/activities/workshops/cc-workshop/

[IETF-84]   http://datatracker.ietf.org/meeting/84/materials.html

[draft-ietf-mmusic-sdp-bundle-negotiation]
    http://tools.ietf.org/html/draft-ietf-mmusic-sdp-bundle-negotiation

[draft-lennox-mmusic-sdp-source-selection]
    http://tools.ietf.org/html/draft-lennox-mmusic-sdp-source-selection

[draft-ietf-sipcore-sip-websocket]   http://tools.ietf.org/id/draft-ietf-sipcore-sip-websocket

[draft-ietf-avtcore-srtp-encrypted-header-ext]
    http://tools.ietf.org/html/draft-ietf-avtcore-srtp-encrypted-header-ext

[draft-muthu-behave-consent-freshness] http://tools.ietf.org/html/draft-muthu-behave-consent-freshness

[draft-westerlund-avtcore-multiplex-architecture]
    http://tools.ietf.org/html/draft-westerlund-avtcore-multiplex-architecture

[draft-westerlund-avtcore-transport-multiplexing]
http://tools.ietf.org/html/draft-westerlund-avtcore-transport-multiplexing

[SILK]   http://developer.skype.com/silk

[CELT]   http://www.celt-codec.org

[draft-spittka-payload-rtp-opus]   http://tools.ietf.org/html/draft-spittka-payload-rtp-opus

[draft-rescorla-random-cname]   http://tools.ietf.org/html/draft-rescorla-random-cname

[draft-perkins-avtcore-rtp-circuit-breakers]   http://tools.ietf.org/html/draft-perkins-avtcore-rtp-circuit-breakers

[draft-ietf-avtext-multiple-clock-rates]   http://tools.ietf.org/html/draft-ietf-avtext-multiple-clock-rates

7 IETF RELATED RFC DOCUMENTS

WebRTC uses a number of IETF standards and protocols documented in Request For Comments (RFCs). These RFCs were not specifically developed for or used by WebRTC.

7.1 Real-time Transport Protocol RFCs

7.1.1 "RTP: A Transport Protocol for Real-Time Applications" [RFC 3550]

RFC 3550 [RFC 3550] defines version 2 of the Real-time Transport Protocol, RTP, and the RTP Control Protocol, RTCP. RTP includes a bit-oriented header field which carries information such as the payload type (codec), timestamp, sequence number, and the synchronization source (SSRC). RTCP messages include Sender Reports (SR), Receiver Reports (RRs), and Source Description (SDES). (Note that the term SDES is an informal name for SDP Security Descriptions, defined in [RFC 4568] – the two concepts are unrelated.) The SDES messages carry the Canonical Name (CNAME) which identifies the user in an RTP session. An RTP mixer can provide information about the senders whose media is included in the packet using the contributing source field (CSRC).

7.1.2 "RTP Profile for Audio and Video Conferences" [RFC 3551]

RFC 3551 [RFC 3551] defines the basic RTP Audio and Video Profile, known as AVP. Formats for a number of common audio and video codecs are defined, along with static payload types (values 0-95). Note that static payload types are no longer allocated – instead dynamic payload types (values 96-127) must be used. This document includes the definition of PCM G.711 audio codec, both A-law and μ-law companding (a portmanteau of compressing and expanding, which results in level compression). This document will need to be updated for use by WebRTC as it recommends DVI4 as an audio codec in addition to G.711.

7.1.3 "The Secure Real-time Transport Protocol (SRTP)" [RFC 3711]

RFC 3711 [RFC 3711] defines the Secure Audio Video Profile for RTP, known as SAVP. This includes the use of Secure RTP (SRTP) and Secure RTCP (SRTCP). SRTP provides confidentiality and authentication to RTP, using symmetric keys to encrypt and decrypt the media and control messages. SRTP uses the Advanced Encryption Standard in Counter Mode, AES-CM. SRTP uses 128 bit keys, although it has been extended to allow 192 and 256 bit keys in [RFC 6188]. SRTP requires a key management protocol to ensure the sender and receiver have the same symmetric key. WebRTC is considering SDP Security Descriptions (SDES) [RFC 4568] and DTLS-SRTP [RFC 5764] as potential key management protocols. SRTP generates an encrypted keystream, which is then Exclusive ORed with the media or control packets to encrypt them. This allows the keystream to be generated in parallel with the media or control packets, resulting in minimum added latency. The encryption is applied to the RTP body, leaving the RTP header in the clear, including RTP header extensions. Authentication is provided by an added authentication tag, which can be 0 to 10 octets in length. Each media stream needs to have a unique session key. If a browser sends two video and two audio streams in a session, there will be four unique session keys used to encrypt them.

7.1.4 "Extended Secure RTP Profile for RTCP-Based Feedback (RTP/SAVPF)" [RFC 5124]

WebRTC uses the Extended Secure RTP Profile for RTCP-Based Feedback [RFC 5124], known as SAVPF. In comparison, most Internet Communications VoIP and video systems today either use the normal Audio Video Profile, AVP, or the Secure Audio Video Profile, SAVP. The SAVPF profile combines the security of SRTP from SAVP [RFC 3711], and the timely feedback of the AVPF profile [RFC 4585]. The basic AVP profile defined in [RFC 3551] includes RTCP feedback messages, and has a mechanism to ensure that excessive bandwidth is not used for these control messages, even for large conferences. One drawback of this is that feedback messages cannot always be sent by the receiver when they would be most useful to the sender. To improve the timeliness of this feedback, AVPF introduces the concept of early RTCP packets and an additional RTCP message known as a feedback message (FB) which can be useful for codecs. The a=rtcp-fb SDP attribute is used to signal which FB messages are to be used. The AVPF profile can interoperate with AVP profiles.

However, SAVP cannot interoperate with AVP profiles, due to the lack of support for best effort encryption.

7.1.5 "Multiplexing RTP Data and Control Packets on a Single Port" [RFC 5761]

This document [RFC 5761] describes how to multiplex RTP and RTCP on the same port. This is done for NAT traversal reasons, minimizing the number times "hole punching" needs to be done. A method to negotiate this in SDP using the attribute a=rtcp-mux is described.

7.1.6 "A Real-time Transport Protocol (RTP) Header Extension for Mixer-to-Client Audio Level Indication" [RFC 6465]

RFC 6465 [RFC 6465] can be used by a mixer in WebRTC to indicate to a WebRTC user agent the audio levels in a mixed audio conference. An audio media mixer receives RTP streams and combines them into a single stream. The mixer usually implements a mixing policy such as the three loudest active speakers. The RTP packet can contain the CSRC (Contributing Source identifiers) indicating which participants contributed to the mixed packet. This RTP header extension adds to this information by providing the audio level of each participant included in the mix. The level is encoded in 7 bits as dBov, which is the level, in decibels, relative to the overload point of the system (the maximum loudness). The presence of this RTP header extension is negotiated using the approach described in [RFC 5285]. This information can be rendered against the conference participant roster, for example, for active speaker identification. This information could have been determined from the participant RTP packet using [RFC 6464].

7.1.7 "A Real-time Transport Protocol (RTP) Header Extension for Client-to-Mixer Audio Level Indication" [RFC 6464]

This specification [RFC 6464] can be used to simplify the operation of a mixer in a WebRTC conference. This RTP extension provides a way for a participant in a conference to indicate the audio level of the packet sent to the mixer. This information is useful for a mixer to quickly select which streams to include in the mix, or a media selector to quickly choose which streams will be selected without having to decode the media packet. The level is encoded in 7 bits as dBov, which is the level, in decibels, relative to the overload point of the system (the maximum loudness). The presence of the RTP header extension is negotiated using the approach described in [RFC 5285]. This information could be copied into a mixed packet using the approach of [RFC 6465].

7.1.8 "Rapid Synchronization of RTP Flows" [RFC 6051]

At the start of an RTP session, there is a period of synchronization between the RTP senders and RTP receivers. For a simple two-party session, this occurs rapidly. However, for multiparty sessions, this can take longer. This document [RFC 6051] discusses the issues in synchronization and redefines RTCP timing and new FB (FeedBack) messages to speed up this process. This could be useful in large multiparty WebRTC sessions.

7.1.9 "RTP Retransmission Payload Format" [RFC 4588]

In cases where the latency requirements of a media stream are not strict, this technique for requesting retransmission of lost RTP packets can be used. The SAVPF profile is necessary, which allows for rapid RTCP FB (FeedBack) packets to be sent. Since WebRTC is about real-time communications, where low latency is necessary, it is far from obvious how this approach could be useful.

7.1.10 "Codec Control Messages in the RTP Audio-Visual Profile with Feedback RTP/AVPF" [RFC 5104]

This document [RFC 5104] describes how to send Codec Control Messages (CCM) using the AVPF profile. These codec control messages can be used for H.271 Video Back Channel, Full Intra Request (FIR), Temporary Maximum Media Stream Bit Rate (TMMBR), and Temporal-Spatial Trade-off. TMMBR can used for congestion control, as discussed in Section 6.4.5. The FIR is used by a video receiver to request that a video sender send an I-frame when video switching has taken place. The ccm parameter is defined for use in the a=rtcp-fb attribute. For example a=rtcp-fb:98 ccm fir would be used to indicate support of FIR CCM for payload 98.

7.1.11 "TCP Friendly Rate Control (TFRC): Protocol Specification" [RFC 5348]

This document [RFC 5348] describes a congestion control mechanism for real-time UDP traffic that shares bandwidth fairly with TCP flows. This mechanism relies on feedback from the receiver to the sender about the packet loss rate and round trip time (RTT). The sender then computes the TCP throughput using the TCP Throughput Equation and adjusts its transmit rate to match this. WebRTC approaches incorporating congestion control will likely make use of this specification.

7.1.12 "A General Mechanism for RTP Header Extensions" [RFC 5285]

The RTP specification [RFC 3550] allows RTP header extensions, but does not specify how to signal or negotiate them or allow more than one extension per RTP packet. This document [RFC 5285] partitions the RTP header extension, allowing for more than one, and describes how they can be signaled using the SDP a=extmap attribute. If RTP header extensions such as [RFC 6464] and [RFC 6465] are used, then this header extension mechanism will be required in WebRTC.

7.1.13 "Guidelines for the Use of Variable Bit Rate Audio with Secure RTP" [RFC 6562]

This document [RFC 6562] discusses issues with variable bit rate encoding (VBR) and encrypted media. Variations in the rate and size of variable bit rate audio packet streams can leak information about the information content, even when encrypted. The use of RTP padding to protect against this is discussed. PCM (G.711) is a constant bit rate (CBR) codec, while Opus can operate in VBR or CBR mode.

7.1.14 "Support for Reduced-Size Real-Time Transport Control Protocol (RTCP): Opportunities and Consequences" [RFC 5506]

This document [RFC 5506] discusses the conditions under which reduced-size RTCP packets (i.e. non-compound packets) can be sent. The use of the a=rtcp-rsize SDP attribute is used to indicate support for reduced-sized RTCP packets. This allows more RTCP packets to be exchanged using the same bandwidth percentage as full-sized RTCP packets. WebRTC uses RTCP feedback for a number of purposes.

7.2 Session Description Protocol RFCs

7.2.1 "SDP: Session Description Protocol" [RFC 4566]

This specification [RFC 4566] defines version 0 of the Session Description Protocol, SDP. SDP session descriptions are used in WebRTC to represent a media stream offer or answer, and is transported and manipulated using JSEP (Section 6.3.7). SDP provides a way to describe media sessions in terms of connection IP address and port, media types, codecs, and configuration information. However, a number of SDP extensions are needed in WebRTC. The SIP usage of SDP to negotiate sessions is known as the offer/answer protocol. The syntax of SDP and SDP extensions is defined using ABNF.

A typical SDP session description from a WebRTC browser is shown in Figure 7.1.

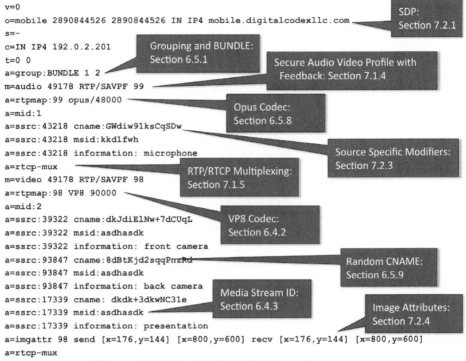

Figure 7.1 SDP with WebRTC Extensions

A minimal SDP session description is shown below, which includes an IPv6 address:

```
v=0
o=alice 2890844526 2890844526 IN IP4 client.digitalcodexllc.com
s=-
c=IN IP6 FF1E:AD32::72EF:8D21:B866
t=0 0
m=audio 49178 RTP/AVP 98
a=rtpmap:98 OPUS/48000
```

A more complicated WebRTC example is shown below, which corresponds to the streams and tracks of Figure 4.1 and the pseudo code of Sections 2.3.1 and 2.3.2. Note that the `a=candidate` lines would not be line wrapped in real SDP.

```
v=0
o=alice 2890844526 2890844526 IN IP4 browserm.example.com
s=-
c=IN IP4 203.0.113.4
t=0 0
a=ice-pwd:asd88fgpdd777uzjYhagZg
a=ice-ufrag:8hhY
a=group:BUNDLE 1 2
m=audio 49178 RTP/SAVPF 99
a=rtpmap:99 opus/48000
a=mid:1
a=ssrc:43218 cname:GWdiw91ksCqSDw
a=ssrc:43218 msid:F8kdls a2
a=ssrc:43218 msid:3dfdf2 a1
a=ssrc:43218 msid:8dFlf a0
a=ssrc:43218 information: microphone
a=rtcp-mux
a=candidate:1 1 UDP 2130706431 192.168.0.5 7381 typ host
a=candidate:2 1 UDP 1694498815 203.0.113.4 49178 typ srflx
raddr 192.168.0.5 rport 7381
m=video 49178 RTP/SAVPF 98
a=rtpmap:98 VP8 90000
a=mid:2
a=ssrc:39322 cname:dkJdiElNw+7dCUqL
a=ssrc:39322 msid:8dFlf v0
a=ssrc:39322 information: front camera
a=ssrc:93847 cname:8dBtKjd2sqqPnzRd
a=ssrc:93847 msid:3dfdf2 v1
a=ssrc:93847 information: back camera
a=ssrc:17339 cname: dkdk+3dkwNC31e
a=ssrc:17339 msid:F8kdls v2
a=ssrc:17339 information: presentation
a=rtcp-mux
a=candidate:1 1 UDP 2130706431 192.168.0.5 17632 typ host
a=candidate:2 1 UDP 1694498815 203.0.113.4 56197 typ srflx
raddr 192.168.0.5 rport 17632
```

7.2.2 "Session Description Protocol (SDP) Bandwidth Modifiers for RTP Control Protocol (RTCP) Bandwidth" [RFC 3556]

This specification [RFC 3556] defines new SDP bandwidth modifiers useful for specifying the bandwidth for RTCP. Normally, RTCP bandwidth is capped at 5% of total bandwidth. The b=RS and b=RR fields defined in this specification allow for direct specification of RTCP senders and RTCP receivers, respectively. Note that b=CT and b=AS are defined in [RFC 4566] and represent the conference total and application specific bandwidth.

7.2.3 "Source-Specific Media Attributes in the Session Description Protocol (SDP)" [RFC 5576]

This specification [RFC 5576] allows for the properties of individual media sources in a stream to be specified in SDP. Note that the term "media stream" is slightly confusing. In some contexts, it means a media object defined in SDP by an m= line. In other contexts, it means a source of RTP packets. In WebRTC, a number of media sources may be associated with a single m= line – this could be multiple streams from the same user, or multiple users contributing streams. This specification defines a media source as an SSRC in RTP. This specification defines the a=ssrc attribute which allows the properties of an SSRC to be declared. Properties such as CNAME (cname), previous SSRC (previous-ssrc), and format-specific parameters (fmtp) are defined. This is being extended, as described in Section 6.5.2, with additional parameters of interest in WebRTC.

7.2.4 "Negotiation of Generic Image Attributes in SDP" [RFC 6236]

This specification [RFC 6236] defines the a=image-attr SDP attribute used to negotiate image attributes. For example, consider:

```
a=imageattr:97 send [x=800,y=640,sar=1.1,q=0.6]
[x=480,y=320] recv [x=330,y=250]
```

This attribute sets for payload 97 the send and receive image sizes, in pixels. For sending, two possible image sizes are offered. The first has a storage aspect ration (sar) of 1.1 and a preference value of 0.6. The second one has the default sar (1.0 for square pixels) and a default preference of 0.5. In addition, the range of acceptable picture aspect ratio (par) can also be set. This is being extended, as described in Section 6.5.2, to allow this to be source specific, which is very important for WebRTC.

7.3 NAT Traversal RFCs

7.3.1 "Interactive Connectivity Establishment (ICE): A Protocol for Network Address Translator (NAT) Traversal for Offer/Answer Protocols" [RFC 5245]

As described in Chapter 4, WebRTC uses Interactive Connectivity Establishment (ICE) [RFC 5245] for NAT traversal and media authorization. ICE is a standardized protocol for "hole punching" - a technique developed in the gaming world to establish a peer-to-peer connection between two hosts behind NAT. Each host gathers potential address candidates: local addresses (read from its NIC, network interface card, interfaces), reflexive addresses (determined from a STUN server), and relay addresses (obtained from a TURN server or other media relay), as shown in Figure 3.8. These candidates are prioritized, encoded as a=candidate lines in SDP, then exchanged using a server located in the public Internet known as a rendezvous server. Both hosts then begin sending test packets, sometimes referred to as "hole punching packets", at roughly the same time. As they attempt to send test packets to the other host's candidate addresses, the packets create NAT mappings and filter rules. In many cases, after a few test packets, an end-to-end path through the NATs is obtained, and this connection is then used for the duration of the session. In some cases, due to strict NAT or firewalls, there is no peer-to-peer connection possible. In this case, the TURN media relay address will be used instead. Non-published statistics from service providers who have used ICE or other similar hole punching approaches report that a direct connection can be obtained up to 85% of the time. A TURN server address could be configured in a web browser in a similar way (and for a similar reason) as a web proxy can be configured in browsers today to enable firewall traversal, as described in Section 3.4.

Since a candidate address in ICE will only be used if an authenticated reply hole punching packet is received from the other host, this provides the media authorization needed. Only if the candidate address is expecting and actively trying to establish a session will the candidate succeed and be used for the session. This prevents the "voice hammer" attack where a candidate address of another host is provided in an attempt to have that host flooded with unwanted traffic.

Connection address candidates are carried in an SDP attribute a=candidate along with the type of address. For example:

```
a=candidate:2 1 UDP 1694498815 192.0.2.3 45664 typ srflx
raddr 10.0.1.1 rport 8998
```

This specification defines the values host, srflx, prflx, and relay for host, server reflexive, peer reflexive, and relayed candidates, respectively.

7.3.2 "Symmetric RTP / RTP Control Protocol (RTCP)" [RFC 4961]

This document [RFC 4916] defines symmetric RTP and RTCP, and provides guidance on when it should be used. RTP is symmetric if packets are sent from the same UDP port to send and receive in a bi-directional RTP session. This is important for traversal of NAT and traversal through TURN and other media relays, such as those provided by SBCs. All media in WebRTC is symmetric as described in Section 3.3.

7.4 References

[RFC 3550]   http://tools.ietf.org/html/rfc3550

[RFC 4568]   http://tools.ietf.org/html/rfc4568

[RFC 3551]   http://tools.ietf.org/html/rfc3551

[RFC 3711]   http://tools.ietf.org/html/rfc3711

[RFC 6188]   http://tools.ietf.org/html/rfc6188

[RFC 5764]   http://tools.ietf.org/html/rfc5764

[RFC 5124]   http://tools.ietf.org/html/rfc5124

[RFC 4585]   http://tools.ietf.org/html/rfc4585

[RFC 5761]   http://tools.ietf.org/html/rfc5761

[RFC 4588]   http://tools.ietf.org/html/rfc4588

[RFC 6465]   http://tools.ietf.org/html/rfc6465

[RFC 5285]   http://tools.ietf.org/html/rfc5285

[RFC 6464]   http://tools.ietf.org/html/rfc6464

[RFC 6051]   http://tools.ietf.org/html/rfc6051

[RFC 4588]   http://tools.ietf.org/html/rfc4588

[RFC 5104]   http://tools.ietf.org/html/rfc5104

[RFC 5104]   http://tools.ietf.org/html/rfc5348

[RFC 5888]   http://tools.ietf.org/html/rfc5888

[RFC 5285]   http://tools.ietf.org/html/rfc5285

[RFC 6562]   http://tools.ietf.org/html/rfc6562

[RFC 5506]   http://tools.ietf.org/html/rfc5506

[RFC 4566]   http://tools.ietf.org/html/rfc4566

[RFC 3556]   http://tools.ietf.org/html/rfc3556

[RFC 5576]   http://tools.ietf.org/html/rfc5576

[RFC 6236]   http://tools.ietf.org/html/rfc6236

[RFC 5245]   http://tools.ietf.org/html/rfc5245

[RFC 4961]   http://tools.ietf.org/html/rfc4961

8 WEBRTC IMPLEMENTATIONS

Web browsers are at various stages of supporting WebRTC APIs and protocols. This information changes rapidly, so always do some searching of official documentation to determine the exact support of WebRTC. This information is presented in alphabetical order.

8.1 Apple Safari

No information yet.

8.2 Google Chrome

Support for getUserMedia and mediastreams is available in Chrome [CHROME] today where it is known as `webkitGetUserMedia()`. These experimental features can be enabled in Google Chrome by entering the URL `chrome://flags` and enabling the PeerConnection features as shown in Figure 8.1. PeerConnection is available in Chrome Canary (Chrome 21 and later) [CANARY] , which implements an early version of JSEP.

8.3 Mozilla Firefox

Firefox [FIREFOX] has shown a demo of Peer Connection at IETF-83 in Paris, but nothing is released yet. Support for `getUserMedia()` is available for Android as a nightly build [MOZILLA-NIGHTLY]. Support for `getUserMedia()` is available for desktop as a special build [MOZILLA-SPECIAL] and will soon be available as a nightly build. It is expected to be generally available in Firefox version 18. The Peer Connection APIs are expected to be generally available in Firefox version 19.

Figure 8.1 Enabling PeerConnection in Google Chrome Canary

8.4 Microsoft Internet Explorer

Microsoft recently published an API document [CU-RTC-WEB]. Discussions about integrating this into the existing standards work are ongoing. As a result, it is not yet clear whether or how much of the existing WebRTC APIs will be supported in Internet Explorer.

8.5 Opera

Opera Mobile 12 [OPERA] has `getUserMedia()` support. Opera has stated they do not intend to support `MediaConstraints`.

8.6 References

[CHROME]   http://www.google.com/chrome

[CANARY]   http://tools.google.com/dlpage/chromesxs

[FIREFOX]   http://www.firefox.com

[MOZILLA-NIGHTLY] http://nightlymozilla.org

[MOZILLA-SPECIAL] http://hg.mozilla.org/projects/alder

[CU-RTC-WEB]   http://html5labs.com/cu-rtc-web/cu-rtc-web.htm

[OPERA]   http://www.opera.com/mobile

APPENDIX A – THE W3C STANDARDS PROCESS

The World Wide Web Consortium is developing the standard APIs for WebRTC. Besides the WEBRTC Working Group, there are a number of other W3C working groups and task groups working on WebRTC.

A.1 Introduction to the World Wide Web Consortium

The World Wide Web Consortium (W3C) [W3C] was established by Tim Berners-Lee, the creator of HTML, to promote the development of HTML and other web technologies. Over time, W3C has built up processes that make it a proper Standards Development Organization (SDO), including a focus on consensus, processes for dispute resolution, handling of non-member comments, implementability testing, permanent storage of and access to discussions, resolutions, and official development drafts of specifications. W3C is a membership organization – only members can create Working Groups, and some Working Groups are restricted such that only members can attend meetings and calls. However, all official documents and final discussions are publicly available on the web without charge. All discussions in the WEBRTC Working Group are public.

Although W3C has a variety of group structures for discussing specifications, only a Working Group leads to an officially sanctioned W3C standard, known as a W3C Recommendation. Recommendations are published in (what else?) HTML format. W3C Working Groups are loosely organized into Activity Domains, but that is primarily for internal W3C administration reasons and has little impact on the direction of the group. In addition, there are Task Forces which are informal collaborations between two or more Working Groups. The Media Task Force that is developing the "Media Capture and Streams" document is one such task force.

The two most important factors in W3C standard development are the specification development stages and the focus on consensus. Specifications in W3C, referred to as Technical Reports, progress through the following stages of maturity:

1) First Public Working Draft
2) Working Draft
3) Last Call Working Draft (LCWD)
4) Candidate Recommendation
5) Proposed Recommendation
6) Recommendation

The first three stages together indicate that a Technical Report is not yet complete technically and does not yet represent broad consensus. The last three stages together indicate that the specification is believed to be technically complete and has had broad review.

More specifically, a specification begins its public life as a First Public Working Draft. At this stage there is no consensus, only an Intellectual Property commitment. There are then any number of Working Drafts released regularly by the Working Group as it hashes out the technical contents of the specification. Although an efficient and effective group will plan to build consensus as it develops these Working Drafts, officially, a Working Draft does not represent consensus and must be cited as a Work in Progress.

Once the Working Group believes a specification is technically complete, it publishes the document as a Last Call Working Draft (LCWD). Interestingly, this is often the first time that other W3C groups will review the draft, so it is not unusual to have more than one LCWD before moving forward. It is also the first time that a record must be kept of the disposition of every public comment - the specification may not move forward until every comment has been addressed to the satisfaction of the commenter, except in unusual circumstances.

After passing the LCWD stage, the next step is to produce a Candidate Recommendation document containing a detailed Implementation Report Plan, which is typically a list of assertions and tests along with a plan for how many implementations of each feature are required in order to progress. The goal at this stage is not to test implementations, but to ensure that there have been enough implementations to confirm that the specification is implementable and, ideally, that implementations will be interoperable. Any specification changes beyond clarifications and editorial changes will cause the document to move back to the Working Draft stage to again ensure sufficient review and consensus. After receiving sufficient implementations according to the plan, and with no major changes needed, the Technical Report can move to the penultimate stage, the Proposed Recommendation. This stage is largely a formality and is, in fact, out of the hands of the Working Group. Assuming there are no public objections within this stage (typically a month), the Report moves automatically to the Recommendation stage.

Any discussion of W3C process would be insufficient if it did not include a discussion of consensus. W3C takes the consensus requirement very seriously, requiring that every objection be addressed if at all possible. Although the IETF only requires rough consensus, W3C requires full consensus. While this can increase the time needed to produce a Recommendation, it reduces the likelihood that the document will knowingly alienates a sizeable fraction of the intended users.

A.2 The W3C WEBRTC Working Group

The main working group in W3C for WebRTC is the WEBRTC Working Group [WEBRTCWG]. Although efforts to create the IETF RTCWEB and the W3C WEBRTC groups began at the same time, it took significantly longer to get the WEBRTC group going. The issue, in this case, was to agree on what to use as a starting document. The WHATWG [WHATWG] is an independent organization that makes suggestions for the direction of HTML development by creating a modification of HTML itself. One such modification was an extension to set up media connections (known as a "Peer Connection") between two browsers. It took a substantial amount of time to work out the copyright issues, but eventually W3C developed a copyright statement that allowed the WEBRTC Working Group to use the WHATWG's PeerConnection text as a starting point for the group's work.

A.3 How WEBRTC relates to other W3C Working Groups

WebRTC's goal is to define APIs for setting up direct browser-to-browser media connections. It is not the goal of WebRTC to define what media is, how media will or could be used by the near or far end, or how it relates to the existing capabilities of HTML. While there are aspects of media synchronization that do need to be defined by WebRTC because of the need to choose synchronized or asynchronous transports, the other aspects listed above are handled by other groups within W3C. Some related groups are listed below.

> Media Capture Task Force [MEDIAWG] - The Media Capture Task Force is comprised of members of two W3C Working Groups: WEBRTC and Device APIs. The goal of this group is to jointly define getUserMedia (), the API call used to request local media (access to a camera, microphone, speaker,

etc.). Additionally, this group will define the core of the MediaStream interface since it is of relevance to both groups.

HTML [HTMLWG] - Clearly the HTML Working Group focuses on the development of the Hyper-Text Markup Language, the language that is the foundation of the World Wide Web. Although there is no direct working relationship between the WEBRTC and HTML WGs, many of the participants in the WEBRTC group are active participants in or followers of the HTML WG. More importantly, WebRTC participants understand that the WebRTC APIs must be consistent with and integrate well with existing HTML APIs and markup. The current version of HTML is HTML5.

Audio [AUDIOWG] - The Audio Working Group develops APIs for more advanced audio manipulation within HTML. Although there is no direct connection between the WEBRTC and Audio WGs, the Audio Working Group has use cases that affect the MediaStream and getUserMedia interfaces being defined by the Media Capture Task Force.

A.4 References

[W3C]   http://www.w3c.org

[WEBRTCWG]   http://www.w3.org/2011/04/webrtc

[WHATWG]   http://www.whatwg.org

[MEDIAWG]   http://www.w3.org/wiki/Media_Capture

[HTMLWG]   http://www.w3.org/html/wg

[AUDIOWG]   http://www.w3.org/2011/audio

APPENDIX B – THE IETF STANDARDS PROCESS

The Internet Engineering Task Force is developing standard protocols for WebRTC. Besides the RTCWEB Working Group, there are a number of other IETF working groups working on WebRTC.

B.1 Introduction to the Internet Engineering Task Force

The Internet Engineering Task Force (IETF) [IETF] is the international standards body responsible for protocol standardization on the Internet. The IETF has standardized protocols such as IP, TCP, UDP, DNS, SIP, RTP, HTTP, and SMTP to name some popular ones. The IETF publishes its standards documents as the numbered series known as "Request for Comments" or RFCs. Note that not all RFCs are IETF documents. Also, not all IETF RFCs are standards documents. Before they are finalized and approved as RFCs, working drafts of standards documents are known as "Internet-Drafts".

Work in the IETF is primarily done over email using mailing lists. There are separate mailing lists for each Working Group. Much of the work on WebRTC in the IETF is discussed in the RTCWEB Working Group, although related work is also happening in other working groups.

There are no membership fees, and anyone can contribute to the work by subscribing to a mailing list, sending comments, writing Internet-Drafts, or attending face-to-face IETF meetings. Work is organized into areas known as Working Groups.

The normal process steps for an IETF document are listed below:

1) Submission of individual Internet-Draft
2) Adoption of a Working Group document
3) Working Group Last Call (WGLC)

4) IETF Last Call
5) Approval by IESG as an RFC.

Internet-Drafts are working documents submitted to the IETF via email or the online form on the IETF website. Internet-Drafts must meet specific formatting requirements and have intellectual property and copyright declarations. Internet-Drafts are frequently updated, and automatically expire after six months if they are not updated or finalized as an RFC. The initial version is -00 (counting from zero) and is incremented for each update. As an individual draft, the authors can include any content they like in their draft. Internet-Drafts are identified by their filename, which always begin "draft-lastname-wgname" where "lastname" is the last name of the principle author or editor, and "wgname" is the name of the working group where the work is likely to be discussed. The rest of the filename is a hyphenated version of the title or content. For example, draft-burnett-rtcweb-constraints-registry is an individual Internet-Draft, written by Daniel C. Burnett for the RTCWEB working group about a constraints registry.

Since WebRTC is a work in progress, many of the documents discussed in this book are Internet-Drafts, and as such their content may have changed. The hyperlinks in this book will automatically take you to the latest version. However, the document name may have changed or documents may have been merged together or split into multiple documents.

Working Groups in the IETF are chartered to produce documents to meet specific protocol milestones. Working Groups "adopt" a draft as a starting point towards producing a consensus document to meet a particular milestone. The authors or editors of the draft are expected to try to reflect working group consensus in the draft from this point on. When the draft is revised, the filename will change to "draft-ietf-wgname", dropping the author name. Since the filename has changed, the version resets to -00. Working group documents tend to get wider review, agenda time at face-to-face IETF meetings, and listings on Working Group pages and summaries.

Once Working Group chairs believe an Internet-Draft is complete and represents the consensus of the group, they will call for a Working Group Last Call (WGLC) for final reviews and comments. If there are significant changes or updates as a result, there may be additional WGLCs for the document. After this process is completed and the chairs believe the draft has "rough consensus" they will move the document towards IETF-wide final review in an IETF Last Call. Upon completion, the members of the Internet Engineering Task Force Steering Committee (IESG) vote. If the vote is successful, the Internet-Draft will be approved and put into the RFC

Editor's queue. After a few months, the draft will be assigned an RFC number and published as an RFC.

There are a number of types of RFCs published by the IETF. The most common are Proposed Standards (PS) and Informational documents. Proposed Standards are actual IETF protocol standards. Informational RFCs do not define protocols or standards but instead document requirements, issues, or the motivation behind protocols. Some WebRTC documents will be published as Informational RFCs, although most will be published as Proposed Standards.

B.2 The IETF RTCWEB Working Group

The main Working Group for WebRTC in the IETF is the RTCWEB Working Group [RTCWEB WG], short for Real-Time Communications Web. However, the WebRTC work encompasses a number of areas, and as such the work is spread across a number of working groups. In addition to Internet-Drafts (working standards documents), WebRTC references other IETF RFCs (Request for Comments, the finished standards documents). Both are also listed and explained in this book.

B.3 How RTCWEB relates to other IETF Working Groups

Besides the work in the RTCWEB Working Group, there is active work relating to WebRTC being done in other working groups, which are listed below.

AVTCORE [AVTCOREWG] - The Audio Video Transport Core Working Group (AVTCORE) standardizes extensions to the Real-time Transport Protocol (RTP), which is used by WebRTC. This is the group responsible for defining how different types of media can be synchronized and sent together.

MMUSIC [MMUSICWG] - The Multiparty Multimedia Session Control Working Group (MMUSIC) standardizes extensions of the Session Description Protocol (SDP), which is used by WebRTC.

CODEC [CODECWG] - The CODEC Working Group is standardizing an Internet audio codec for speech and music known as Opus. The Opus codec will be the default audio codec used by WebRTC.

SIPCORE [SIPCOREWG] - The Session Initiation Protocol Core Working Group is involved in the ongoing maintenance and extensions to the core SIP protocol. One chartered item is a WebSocket transport for SIP, which would allow SIP to be used with WebRTC systems. SIP can also be used as a signaling protocol between web servers in the WebRTC trapezoid shown in Figure 1.5.

B.4 References

[IETF]   http://www.ietf.org

[RTCWEBWG]   http://tools.ietf.org/wg/rtcweb

[AVTCOREWG]   http://tools.ietf.org/wg/avtcore

[MMUSICWG]   http://tools.ietf.org/wg/mmusic

[CODECWG]   http://tools.ietf.org/wg/codec

[SIPCOREWG]   http://tools.ietf.org/wg/sipcore

APPENDIX C – GLOSSARY

ABNF – Augmented Backus-Naur Format. This is the meta-language used to define the syntax of text-based Internet protocols such as SDP and URLs. Originally defined in RFC 822, the most recent specification is RFC 5234.

API – Application Programming Interface. APIs are interfaces used by software components to communicate with each other.

HTML5 – The latest version of Hyper-Text Markup Language, the markup language used on the World Wide Web for web pages and applications. HTML originally defined simple markup tags in XML. Today, HTML5 supports Cascading Style Sheets (CSS) and scripting such as JavaScript. WebRTC is the part of HTML5 that deals with real-time voice, video, and data streams in browsers.

JavaScript – An interpreted scripting programming language used on web pages. Despite the name, it is quite different from Java. Today, most advanced web pages and applications use JavaScript. Technically, JavaScript is an implementation of the ECMA-262 (ECMAScript) standard. In practice, the terms JavaScript and ECMAScript are used interchangeably.

Jingle – A multimedia signaling protocol, which is an extension of XMPP (Extensible Messaging and Presence Protocol, RFC 6120, also known as Jabber). Jingle is defined by XEP-0166. Jingle uses RTP/SRTP for media, ICE NAT traversal, and supports mapping of media information to SDP.

NAT - Network Address Translation. NAT is a function often built into Internet routers or hubs that map one IP address space to another space. Usually, NATs are used to allow a number of devices to share an IP address, such as in a residential router or hub. NATs are also used by enterprises or service providers to segment IP networks, simplifying control and administration. Many Internet protocols, especially those using TCP transport or a client/server architecture, have no difficulty traversing NATs. However, peer-to-peer protocols and protocols using UDP transport can have major difficulties. NAT traversal in WebRTC uses the ICE protocol. For details of how NAT and hole punching works, see Chapter 10 of SIP: Understanding the Session Initiation Protocol, 3rd Edition. NAT is also sometimes used to refer to Network Address Translator, the device that implements the NAT function.

Offer/Answer – Media negotiation is the way in which two parties in a communication session, such as two browsers, communicate and come to agreement on an acceptable media session. Offer/answer is an approach to media negotiation in which one party first sends to the other party what media types and capabilities it supports and would like to establish – this is known as the "offer". The other party then responds indicating which of the offered media types and capabilities are supported and acceptable for this session – this is known as the "answer". This process can be repeated a number of times to setup and modify a session. While the term offer/answer is general, when used in WebRTC, it usually refers to RFC 3264 which defined the Offer/Answer Protocol, a usage of SDP by SIP. Offer/Answer must be studied in order to understand how exchanging SDP session descriptions can be used to negotiate a media session with WebRTC. For examples of SDP offer/answer, see Chapter 13 of SIP: Understanding the Session Initiation Protocol, 3rd Edition.

Peer Connection – This term is used to refer to a direct connection set up between two "peers", two web browsers in the context of WebRTC, for the purpose of transporting audio, video, and data. Such a connection is established using

132

the `RTCPeerConnection` and related APIs.

SIP – Session Initiation Protocol. SIP is an application level signaling protocol used for Internet Communications, Voice over IP, and video. SIP is defined by RFC 3261 and uses SDP session descriptions as defined by the offer/answer protocol.

WebSocket – The WebSocket protocol establishes bi-directional TCP connections between a web browser and a web server. The connection opening is signaled by the browser using HTTP, and can stay open until either side closes it.

APPENDIX D – SUPPLEMENTARY READING AND SOURCES

For background on HTML5 and JavaScipt, we recommend the easy-to-follow tutorials at:

http://www.w3schools.com

For background on an Internet communication signaling protocol such as Session Initiation Protocol, we recommend:

Johnston, Alan B, SIP: Understanding the Session Initiation Protocol, Artech House, Boston, 2009, 283 pages, 3rd Edition. ISBN-13:978-1607839958

This book also discusses NAT traversal and hole punching, SDP session descriptions, and SDP offer/answer.

Sinnreich, Henry and Alan B. Johnston, Internet Communications using SIP: Delivering VoIP and Multimedia Services with Session Initiation Protocol (Networking Council Series), John Wiley and Sons, New York, 2005, 298 pages, 2nd Edition. ISBN-13:978-0471776574

For background on RTP and media transport, we recommend:

Perkins, Colin, RTP: Audio and Video for the Internet, Addison-Wesley Professional, New York, 2003, 432 pages.

ISBN-13:978-0672322495

For Internet Communications security for VoIP and video, we recommend:

Johnston, Alan B. and D. Piscitello, <u>Understanding Voice over IP
Security</u> , Artech House, Boston, 2006, 276 pages,   ISBN-
13: 978-1596930506

For an entertaining fictional account of cybercrime and hacking that also
happens to teach the basics of computer and Internet security, we
recommend:

Johnston, Alan B, <u>Counting from Zero</u>, 2011, 281 pages,
paperback ISBN-13:978-1461064886 or Kindle eBook

INDEX

ABOUT THE AUTHORS

Dr. Alan B. Johnston has over thirteen years of experience in SIP, VoIP (Voice over IP), and Internet Communications, having been a co-author of the SIP specification and a dozen other IETF RFCs, including the ZRTP media security protocol. He is the author of four best selling technical books on Internet Communications, SIP, and security, and a techno thriller novel "Counting from Zero" that teaches the basics of Internet and computer security. He is on the board of directors of the SIP Forum. He holds Bachelors and Ph.D. degrees in electrical engineering. Alan is an active participant in the IETF RTCWEB working group. He is currently a Distinguished Engineer at Avaya, Inc. and an Adjunct Instructor at Washington University in St Louis. He owns and rides a number of motorcycles, and enjoys mentoring a robotics team.

Dr. Daniel C. Burnett has more than a dozen years of experience in computer standards work, having been author and editor of the W3C standards underlying the majority of today's automated Interactive Voice Response (IVR) systems. He has twice received the prestigious "Speech Luminary" award from Speech Tech Magazine for his contributions to standards in the Automated Speech Recognition (Voice Recognition) field. As an editor of the PeerConnection and getUserMedia W3C WEBRTC specifications and a participant in the IETF, Dan has been involved from the beginning in this exciting new field. He is currently the Director of Standards at Voxeo. When he can get away, Dan loves camping both with his family and with his son's Boy Scout Troop.

Follow Alan and Dan on Twitter as @alanbjohnston and @danielcburnett and on Google+ as alanbjohnston@gmail.com danielcburnett@gmail.com.

For information on future editions along with updates and changes since publication, visit http://webrtcbook.com

Facebook http://www.facebook.com/webrtcbook
Google+ http://plus.google.com/102459027898040609362

Also by Alan B. Johnston:
Counting from Zero

Can a security expert save the Internet from a catastrophic zero day cyber attack by a network of zombie computers, known as a botnet? At what cost? Unfolding across three continents, this novel gives a realistic insider's view of the thrust and parry world of computer security and cryptography, and the very real threat of botnets.

"Credible and believable, this story is told by a subject matter expert. I could not wait to find out what happened next."
- Vint Cerf, Internet pioneer

"The threat to the Internet from worms, viruses, botnets, and zombie computers is real, and growing. **Counting from Zero** is a great way to come up to speed on the alarming state of affairs, and Johnston draws you in with his story and believable cast of characters."
- Phil Zimmermann, creator of Pretty Good Privacy (PGP) the most widely used email encryption program

"**Counting from Zero** brings Dashiell Hammet and Raymond Chandler into the computer age."
- Diana Lutz

Made in the USA
San Bernardino, CA
30 November 2012